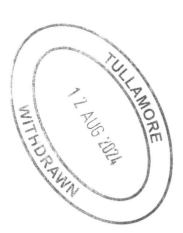

D1615581

Silent Sentinels

Silent Sentinels

Donal MacCarron

NONSUCH

I gcuimhine m'athair agus mo mhátair grádhmhar.

To the memory of my parents,
Maura (*née* Collins) and James MacCarron.

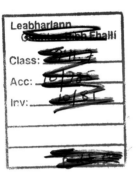
First published 2008

Nonsuch Publishing
73 Lower Leeson Street
Dublin 2, Ireland
www.nonsuchireland.com

© Donal MacCarron, 2008

The right of Donal MacCarron to be identified as the Author
of this work has been asserted in accordance with the
Copyrights, Designs and Patents Act 1988.

British Library Cataloguing in Publication Data.
A catalogue record for this book is available from the British Library.

ISBN 978 1 84588 923 4

Typesetting and origination by Nonsuch Publishing.

Contents

Acknowledgements

Whenever I approach the task of thanking people for the help they have given with my various research activities, I always have a frisson of doubt! Suppose I was to leave out any helpful person, particularly should he or she have contributed magnanimously to the cause? Therefore, having made my excuses for a sometimes dodgy memory up front, I now have great pleasure in listing the following …

In Co. Donegal I am greatly indebted to Col. Declan O'Carroll, and to Col. Brian O'Reilly who were, together with others, the moving spirits behind the excellent museum that has been enjoyed at Fort Dunree for the past twenty-two years. Both are based in Letterkenny, as is another retired army man, Jim Gallagher, who provided some excellent hard-to-trace photographs of Lenan. Col. Jim Prendergast, now living in Mullingar, also contributed to setting up the Dunree facilities and fielded many of my awkward questions with great patience. The curator of the Dunree Museum, David McGee is worthy of a special mention because, inter alia, he provided many good colour photographs of his charges. Now living in Naas, Col. Gerry Swan, a gunner, gave me a detailed education in the mysteries of big guns! Also living in Co. Kildare is Mark McLoughlin whose grandfather served in the Cork forts shortly after the end of the Great War and eventually became a colonel in our own army.

Though I visited the Cork forts with other members of the Military

History Society of Ireland some twenty years ago, this is my first opportunity to remember with gratitude that late Lieutenant Sean O'Brien of the Irish Naval Service who made that two-day trip memorable for everyone. Unfortunately Sean could not show us Fort Meagher (Fort Camden as was) because of various restrictions and it is to be hoped that the present owners, Cork County Council, will at last allow access to one of the finest examples of coastal forts. One of the group on that visit was Dr Pat McCarthy who was a great help with reference to the war in the Atlantic, and Sean Healy for his excellent photography highlighting the present pitiful state of the Cork forts.

While in the Cork area, as it were, I must thank Comdt Mick Dowling of the 1st Southern Brigade (my guide on a much later visit), Comdt Mick Hartigan and Comdt Brian Parsons (his collection of aerial views of the forts can now be enjoyed by all comers). In the reserve forces, with which I can personally identify, are those members of the Southern Command FCA who, at the end of the war, were formed into a coastal defence battery before becoming a field unit. Among their members were Joe Standen and Liam Plante – 'jildy files' every one! Older members of the forts' garrisons who served during the Emergency years are Bill Walsh and in particular John Treacy, whose recollections of the great ceremonies of 1938 were taken direct from his own lips.

Turning to the ladies: Carmel Dineen of the Port of Cork and Dawn Fairweather of Crawford Art Gallery, gave unstinting help with the historic paintings shown in this volume. The staff of the Army Archives in Cathal Brugha Barracks, Dublin, were, as ever, most helpful and I can say the same for the people at the Royal Arsenal Library at Woolwich, London. On the subject of art: let me pay my respects to a brilliant naval artist, Kenneth King in his seaside studio in Glencolmcille.

I hope this book will be a tribute of all the generations who served the guns in the forts and the unwilling but hard-working men who were forced to build the forts in darker days. They were not the only prisoners to be held in Spike Island because so too, generations later, were many of the brave men interned there during the dangerous days of the War of Independence. I am glad to record the help given by Mary and Michael Carrig of Tarbert and Sean Swords of Wicklow in connection with our own 'home-built' Fort Shannon. Thanks also to Adrian English and Glenn Thompson, military historians both.

In the UK, I received unstinting co-operation from Deglan de Cogan and from two members of the Fortress Study Group, Col. Bill Clements and Charles Blackwood, who edits Casemate, the journal of that group, and Geoff Hallett, secretary of the Palmerston Forts Society. I must record my thanks to the ladies of Gerrards Cross Library for their diligence in sourcing reference books.

As with all of my work, the computer expertise of my wife Monique was invaluable, and her patience inexhaustible.

D. M. MacC.
Gerrards Cross
November 2008

Introduction

This year marks the seventieth anniversary of a crucial development in Irish history which has long been neglected by historians. In the pre-war summer of 1938, as a result of negotiations between the Government of Éire and that of the United Kingdom, seven coastal forts that had remained in British hands since the articles of agreement, commonly called the Treaty, of 1921, were returned. Had these fortifications, known as the Treaty forts, remained in British hands, then the Irish State would have been unable to maintain its oft-declared neutrality in the event of a continental war between the great powers.

Not only did the Treaty allow for British occupation in peacetime, but it also required 'such other facilities as may from time to time be agreed between the two governments'. And, crucially, 'in time of war or strained relations with a foreign power, such harbour and other facilities as the British Government may require'! There, as Shakespeare wrote, was the rub.

As matters settled down between the two nations, Britain looked to Ireland to pay for its own coast defences and strictly limited naval forces, as was the case with other British dominions. William T. Cosgrave, then President of the Irish Executive Council, said that the government would eventually do likewise, but he stressed that the infant state was faced with a bill of £500,000 to repair the damage to the country's infrastructure caused by the Civil War. The reader can probably work out this figure in today's money … it is a huge amount!

What happened in the event was that from 1921 until 1938 one of the Royal Navy's destroyers, referred to as 'the guardship', could be seen at the Admiralty moorings opposite Cobh, with its White Ensign fluttering in the breeze. Like the Union flags in the coastal forts, this panoply no doubt was a pleasant sight to the old ascendancy – but was anathema to most others. This scene in Cork's great harbour was repeated at the two forts guarding Donegal's deep anchorage of Lough Swilly with gunners of the Royal Artillery, together with supporting elements of Royal Engineers and Royal Signals, remaining on post until the heady days of the summer of 1938.

The story of these forts goes back 400 years in time, when Henry VIII was the Tudor Lord of Ireland. Henry was very conscious of guarding his realm against France and Spain and he demonstrated this by virtually founding the Royal Navy. Neither did he neglect the ports from which his galleons sailed and he saw that these too were defended by castles. His daughter and successor, Elizabeth I, had to contend with the Spanish Armada pre 1588 and she too was conscious of the need to maintain and expand Henry's ring of castles. She used Bere Island as a staging post for her troops who were attempting to put down the rebellious Irish in campaigns which culminated in the defeat of the old Gaelic Order at Kinsale in 1601. Thereafter, as artillery improved both on ships and on shore (Henry VIII had introduced big guns to Ireland during his reign), the importance or neglect of coast defences waxed and waned in keeping with the political situation. Down the years there was a continuous battle, best described as 'keeping up with the Joneses'. As guns and armour on warships improved, so did the deterrent equipment in the coastal forts.

The Second World War erupted on 1 September 1939 and quickly became a worldwide conflagration that did not end until August of 1945. The seven Treaty forts located in Cork Harbour and Bantry Bay and Lough Swilly in Donegal had been of prime strategic value to Britain during the Great War and these, together with the port facilities, would have been available to Great Britain had a new Agreement in 1938 not been negotiated. This Agreement returned ports and forts completely and unambiguously to Irish sovereignty. Despite this solemn agreement, when the Second World War broke out, Great Britain wanted these facilities returned and demanded the restoration of their 1921 status. Éire, as the Irish Free State had been renamed by the new Constitution of 1937, would have none of it and relations between the two countries teetered on the brink of war.

Chapter 1

A Safe Harbour for Ships

If you should sail into Cork Harbour, maybe on the ferry, or perhaps steering your yacht, you will see on the port bow Fort Camden and shortly thereafter, on the starboard side, Fort Carlisle, both still standing, as they have done for centuries. In troubled times the forts have added strength to the motto in Latin on the arms of Cork City, 'A Safe Harbour for Ships'. Originally this referred to the gift bestowed by Nature, the best-sheltered harbour in Ireland. From the thirteenth century, a considerable and growing trade with Europe developed and Irish traders were well known in France, Spain, the Low Countries and Italy. The busy activity of the crowded port was rendered by an unknown poet:

> Where rising masts and endless prospect yield,
> With labour burn, and echo to the shouts
> Of hurry'd sailor as he heartily waves
> His last adieu, and loosening every sheet,
> Resigns the spreading vessel to the wind.

A contemporary photograph of the entrance to Fort Mitchel. It demonstrates the skill of the convicts who were incarcerated in a prison on Spike Island in earlier times.

The prosperity of Cork and its harbour was attractive to English merchants who used political power to curtail and usurp this valuable trade. To guard this strategic port a number of coast defences were built, because these times saw Spain, England, Holland and France struggle for both naval and mercantile supremacy.

For Cromwell, the harbour became the principal re-victualling port for his Roundheads deployed in the brutal subjugation of south-west Ireland. The coast of Co. Cork was subjected to increasing attacks by Turkish and Algerian pirates, but though there was a strong military presence in the area this did not prevent frequent raids by buccaneers, as commemorated in 'The Sack of Baltimore'.

Later, Britain found herself threatened by Europe, but most actively by France and Spain. Though her armies were defeated on land in the American War of Independence, the new nation's dashing privateer John Paul Jones, was still at large around her coasts. In the years

1778-9, he brazenly raided Whitehaven Harbour, spiked all its coast guns, and burnt all the vessels lying at anchor there. He then slipped across the Irish Sea and, keeping carefully out of the range of the guns of Carrickfergus, he captured HMS *Drake* and her twenty cannon. He was still causing trouble in the North Sea in the autumn of 1779. Conscious of all these dangers, though there was general peace in 1783, the War Office began to install garrisons and batteries on Spike Island, at the old sites of Fort Camden and Fort Carlisle and near Roche's Tower at the harbour entrance. The main armament was 24-pounders with a considerable number of smaller weapons, an imposing array of guns which was kept up to strength, ready for the resumption of the war with France in 1803.

The harbour was used increasingly in the late 1700s, both as a naval base and as a port for cargo vessels bound across the North Atlantic and to the West Indies. Further in from the mouth of the harbour lies Spike Island, described as a 'breakwater' to the final channel to Cork Harbour; it deserves this description because at this point, visiting vessels must turn sharply westward for the final leg to the docks. The island masks the old naval base at Queenstown, the name given to commemorate the landing there of Queen Victoria in 1849 and used to describe not only the naval base at this point, but the whole of the great harbour.

The earliest record of Spike Island tells how the then King of Munster gifted the island to St Carthage of Lismore for healing his many ailments. The holy man built a monastery there and spent a year overseeing its construction. When he departed he left behind forty of his brethren and their piety inspired this description of the island, 'a most holy place and most holy people resided there in perpetuity'. All this happened in the seventh century but thereafter the record of Spike is a complete blank until the twelfth century, when the monastery was destroyed by ruthless Danish raiders who frequently landed in the harbour and ravaged the surrounding countryside. Their forays ended when they were converted to Christianity and settled peacefully in Cork City about the year 850.

A millennium passed on Spike, which one historian succinctly compressed as follows, 'In the course of time, it had degenerated, becoming in turn a haunt of smugglers, an uninhabited place, a fortress, a penal establishment, and, finally, that which it now forms – an army depot peopled only by the numerous soldiers who garrison it under the sonorous military title of Fort Westmoreland.' The author, writing at the end of the nineteenth century and using the flowery language of the time, brought the island's history right up-to-date:

> There is no island within the circuit of the British Isles which can lay claim to such a chequered, albeit uneventful, history as the little island called Spike, in Cork Harbour. A splendid natural breakwater to Cork Harbour, its green, battery-crowned slopes is the first land sighted by the homeward-bound mariner; and affords all but 'the last glimpse of Erin that in sorrow is seen" by the departing Irish emigrant, or the Irish soldier sailing away in a great white trooper to guard our distant India or colonial possessions'.

The name of the fort had come from the Lord Lieutenant of Ireland, who had visited the island in 1790 and on departing gave the workers 100 guineas. In 1804 an average of £4,000 per month was being spent on Spike and by 1812 the overall cost reached £1 million. In July 1805 Spike was visited by Arthur Wellesley (later to become the Duke of Wellington) as part of his tour of military works in the south and west of the country. In the following year he was appointed chief secretary for Ireland, a post he held until 1809.

By 1860 the completion of Spike at Fort Westmoreland was under the direction of a very capable army engineer who was so taken by Ireland that he asked a stonemason to teach him the Gaelic language. An Englishman of Huguenot extraction, he delved deeply into the history and the antiquities of Ireland. As a tribute to his wide interests, his portrait is hung in the library of the Royal Dublin Society. His successor continued to superintend the works on Spike and on the two other forts, Camden and Carlisle near the mouth of the harbour, which were being improved.

Before this, a convict prison had been established in Fort Westmoreland and for many years it supplied convict labour for the development of the harbour forts. At one stage the prison held over 2,000 men, many of them political prisoners. At first they were crowded together in large barrack rooms, which they eventually divided with corrugated iron partitions and wire netting into separate sleeping cells at a cost of £4 per cell. In 1862, a report 'on the treatment of convicts in Ireland' was issued by four visiting justices of the West Riding Prison in Yorkshire. In this, the directors of the prison complained of the misappropriation of labour 'by which men are set to do the work of horses' and also of other 'inconveniences'. These arose because prison management was split between two government departments, one answerable for moral control and training of the convicts, the other for the execution of work.

The convicts' diet, per head, per week, consisted of 13 ounces of bread, 2 ounces of meat, 1 pound 6½ ounces of rice, 4 pints of soup, 7 pints of gruel and 10¼ pints of milk – hardly sufficient for the hard work of quarrying and dressing stone, and other heavy building work. Many of the political prisoners were awaiting transportation to Australia but several managed to escape from the new colony to America and became a factor to be reckoned with, both in that country and when they eventually returned to Ireland. In time, three of them gave their names to the three forts of Cork Harbour.

The English writer quoted earlier finished his description of Spike as follows:

It is hoped that its formidable cannon may never be employed save for such pacific purposes as celebrating the Sovereign's birthday, or saluting such friendly foreign potentates as from time-to-time arrive in Cork Harbour

– planted at whose mouth, for its safety and protection in more ways than one, stands so providentially the green and storied island of Spike.

A cosy loyal ending indeed.

Fort Westmoreland on Spike is a fine example of bastion design: it is the only one of its kind which has been permanently occupied to this day. The architecture here and at the other harbour forts in their final nineteenth-century appearance is one of monumental character, with carefully constructed masonry. Alas, by the beginning of the twentieth century, stonework gave way to mass concrete construction of little architectural merit. Thereafter, modern coastal defence installations consisted of open gun positions backed by ancillary structures, practical but prosaic.

Some five miles to the west of Cork City, Ballincollig gunpowder mills were established in the 1790s. Eventually there were sixteen gunpowder mills here making charcoal, refining sulphur and saltpetre, drying the resulting gunpowder mix, and making casks to take the product. The mills' output by 1837 was 16,000 barrels annually – so the cannon guarding the harbour at Cork were never short of propellant.

Chapter 2

The Twin Forts

Thomas Davis, a Young Irelander, was twenty years of age when the Treaty fort that now bears his name was rebuilt, but no doubt the ancestors of this Corkman had stood on the site generations before. This was borne out by surveyors who found traces of earlier defences there. Their survey was in preparation for a state-of-the-art fortification of large rectangular design with platforms for gun batteries down at sea level. During the Williamite Wars in Ireland, an earlier fort had been garrisoned by troops loyal to James II until they were driven out by William's army in September 1690. Its commander, the Duke of Marlborough, then proceeded on his victorious way occupying Haulbowline Island *en route* to an easy victory over Shandon Castle and Cork City itself.

Much later, when the French Revolutionary Wars erupted and were followed by the Emperor Napoleon's campaigns, Carlisle's garrison stood to its guns lest an invading French force appeared. However the only French soldiers who eventually got into the fort were innocuous prisoners-of-war taken in various engagements. The fort as it stands today dates from 1860, a time when the harbour perimeter was busy

Seen from a boat, Fort Meagher looks harmless enough, though it once was a major deterrent to vessels attempting to pass into Cork Harbour.

with construction works here, across the water at Camden, further inwards at Spike Island, and on its neighbouring island, Haulbowline.

The first contractors at Carlisle laboured throughout 1860 on preparatory work, principally the excavation of a main defensive ditch and the formation of a stone parapet – the soil taken from the ditch was used to flatten an area which would become the parade ground. The prepared site was handed over to a main contractor in August 1861, who carried on until the end of the following year when he realised that he had underpriced the job. The War Office pressurised him into fulfilling the contract but the unhappy man filed for bankruptcy and the job was handed over to a new firm, which worked steadily until the autumn of 1863. Still not satisfied, the War Office took the task over itself.

It had the option of using unpaid convicts from Spike Island. A group of twenty prisoners began by repairing the existing approach roads but no real progress was made on actual defences until the early summer of 1864 when an increased number of convicts began to dig out foundations for the lower sea batteries. The number of the unfortunate convicts was increased further until there were altogether 180 men working on site. At a quarry on the mainland, still known as the Convicts' Quarry, they undertook the back-breaking work of winning stone for the lower sea batteries, already excavated. Next the workers laid concrete foundations for gun platforms and built magazines, storage for small arms and ammunition, and the landward walls. Many convicts had learnt how to dress the stone they quarried and their excellent work can be seen to this day. In the latter half of 1867 they were reinforced by infantrymen, but at the end of the year all were withdrawn. However, there was no rest for the convicts, as they were transferred to building new naval dockyards at Haulbowline.

Work resumed at Carlisle when a party of Royal Marines and Royal Engineers, together with forty-five civilians, began construction of huts on the central parade ground, which would provide accommodation for further increases in the military working party. Though the convicts were unpaid, the work to date had cost £10,000 and it was reckoned that a further £115,000 would be needed to complete Carlisle and that this would take ten more years to achieve.

A new frontage on the landward side, together with a barracks, was completed in 1864. Next, new batteries at both high level and sea level were built and amongst the guns positioned there were three 7-inch ones mounted on 'disappearing' carriages. In 1870 *The Irish Builder* reported:

> The outer defences of Camden and Carlisle which command the entrance to the magnificent harbour of Queenstown are being pushed forward rapidly. An infantry regiment encamped on the heights above Camden is employed daily in sinking new trenches and carrying out other works, some of which are on a stupendous scale. Each fort is now virtually cut off from the mainland by a wide ditch fully 40 feet deep. Besides this, means are provided for working under cover. Large batteries of heavy guns completely

This photograph, taken at Fort Davis, shows a 6-inch gun in fairly good state in 1988 …

hidden from view can, whenever required, open a destructive fire upon approaching vessels and annihilate a hostile fleet before it can pass through the harbour entrance between the two forts. The convict labour has been turned to account upon the new government dockyards at Haulbowline.

In 1880 'casemates', virtually all-round protected positions, were excavated in the face of the cliffs and equipped with nine rifled muzzle-loading guns ranging from 7-inch to 11-inch in calibre. Calibre denoted the circumference of the muzzle and this description had taken over from poundage as a measurement for weapons. These constituted a formidable array of big guns in virtually impregnable positions. By 1890 the guns at Carlisle and at Camden and elsewhere in the Empire, were a mixture of older guns and new quick-firing breech-loaders. Still to be seen at Carlisle are segmental arches of carefully-dressed masonry spanning the gun openings and the iron shields which can close off the embrasures.

At the west side of the harbour mouth a headland known as Ram's

… The same gun at Fort Davis rusting away twenty years later.

Head had been the site for various coastal defences from the mid-1500s. Its name, incidentally, does not refer to a male sheep, rather it is an anglicised version of 'Rinn Reanhar', meaning a stout point. In the Williamite Wars, forces loyal to James II occupied the harbour and fortified this ancient site with two blockhouses mounting eight guns. When William's fleet approached, these guns opened fire – it was to be the only time this fort, throughout its long history, ever fired a shot in anger.

The name of the Earl of Camden, who was Lord Lieutenant of Ireland, was bestowed on the fort – luckily this was not the nobleman's given name, which was John Pratt! Improvements continued apace in the fort during the uneasy period of peace with France which ended in 1793. The landward side was remodelled to take thirty guns, in addition to an existing battery of twelve heavy guns on the seaward side. Towards the end of the century the Royal Garrison Artillery still manned the fort but was replaced by the 33rd Company of Royal Engineers – this change

This beautifully crafted staircase in Fort Davis remains as a memorial to the unfortunate convicts who built it.

from gunners to sappers underlines what was happening to artillery. In a relatively short period, smooth-bore muzzle-loading cannon had progressed to quick-firing breech-loaders. Range had vastly increased up to 17,000 yards and accuracy had correspondingly improved. Concurrently, of course, the guns on warships standing far out to sea were also more powerful. Fort Camden, with its weaponry reduced to eight 12-pounders, had nevertheless a new and highly important role.

Observing warships at night presented a problem that was not resolved until 1860 when the electric arc light had been developed. Now, targets could be illuminated up to four-and-a-half miles away in clear conditions. By 1900 the standard searchlight was the 60-inch, this being the measurement of its lens's diameter. To protect the lights from enemy action they were installed in concrete or brick-work enclosures. The powerful searchlights at Fort Camden were manned by army engineers; they remained giving valuable service until conventional coastal defences disappeared. The task of long-range counter-bombardment was now entrusted to a new battery further south on the coast at Templebreedey, equipped with a pair of powerful 9.2-inch guns.

Chapter 3

The Brennan Torpedo

A unique weapon installed at Fort Camden was the brainchild of a mechanical genius, Louis Philip Brennan, born in Co. Mayo in 1852. His family emigrated to Australia when he was nine years of age. Later he studied in Melbourne University, where his inventive talents were developed.

In 1874 Brennan invented the dirigible torpedo, which has been called 'the first guided missile'. This system consisted of a large steam-driven winch with the free end of its cable attached to a conventionally shaped explosive torpedo. Inside this the cable was tightly wound around a drum which, when the winch was operated, would rotate and drive the torpedo's propellers. Once launched along guide rails to a depth of 10ft, the torpedo would be steered by an operator perched high in the fort with a clear view of possible targets. He followed the weapon's course by its short mast protruding out of the water. He was further aided by a special light that produced smoke by day and flames by night. By varying the rate at which the wires on both drums rotated, the operator could alter both the speed and direction of the torpedo to guide it to the target. A differential fitted between the winch ashore

Louis Brennan (1852 - 1932) – Prolific inventor, born in Co. Mayo. (*Courtesy of C.D. Blenhiem-Whitmore.*)

and the drum afloat activated the torpedo's rudder. For the first time in military history a weapon had been devised which could be guided all the way to its target.

The Brennan torpedo was introduced at a favourable time, as much energy was being devoted to the protection of naval bases, and the War Office's decision to adopt this revolutionary concept highlights its faith in the weapon and the strategic importance of Cork Harbour, where it was introduced in great secrecy. Over its years in service, from 1888 until 1904 when it was superseded by improvements to 9.2-inch guns, minimum stocks of 200 torpedoes were held.

Brennan produced many other practical innovations, a major one being a transport system. In Australia, he was struck by the difficulties and costs of building railways through hilly but sparsely-populated areas which would produce little revenue. He conceived the idea of a

The Brennan guided torpedo was 24ft in length. Here, a surviving example shows the nose cone which was packed with 300lbs of explosive, and behind it, the body of the weapon. (*Courtesy of J.S. Earle,* Defence Lines.)

self-propelling vehicle which could travel on a single railway line and remain safely upright. That was the principle behind his Gyroscopic Monorail. This device became the sensation of the Japan–Britain Exhibition in London in 1910 and it won the Exhibition's highest award, attracting the attention of many senior government figures.

Other ideas were: an early helicopter which could both fly and hover; a two-wheeled Gyrocar which was acknowledged as being more comfortable and safer than the conventional car; and a long list which included a five-character silent typewriter, chicken incubators, mincing machines, soldering rods, wool clippers and food-packing machines. Many of these were adopted commercially, but it was his guided torpedo which stood out from all his extraordinary work and was a major personal financial success. In addition to Fort Camden, the system was installed in other coastal forts in the UK and elsewhere, includ-

In June 1889 Louis Brennan demonstrated his torpedo mounted in the Cliff End Battery, Isle of Wight. He demolished the target vessel SS *Monarch*. (*Courtesy of R.E. Museum, Chatham.*)

ing far-flung outposts of the Empire like Hong Kong. In 1922 Ireland honoured him by his inclusion among 120 distinguished people who were invited to become foundation members of a proposed National Academy of Ireland.

Louis Brennan was recovering from an illness in Montreux, Switzerland, when, in December 1931, he was knocked down by a car; the ultimate irony for the inventor of the safer Gyrocar. He died from his injuries a fortnight later, just eleven days short of his eightieth birthday. The remains of the launching rails can still be seen in Fort Camden and in two overseas forts. Had Cork Harbour been infiltrated at night, the following scenario can be imagined: a stealthy warship approaching the harbour is suddenly revealed by the powerful searchlights of Fort Camden. Its crew, taken aback and blinded, are unaware of the smoking torpedo which is on its way to greet them!

Chapter 4

Berehaven

At the head of broad Bantry Bay lies Bere Island, guarding the harbour of Castletown Berehaven. The island is about five miles long and three miles at its broadest point; the width of the channel of water between it and the mainland varies from 300 yards at the western end to 1200 yards at the eastern end where there is an entrance easy of access. Berehaven, at the time of Elizabeth I, was a support base for her armies who were busy fighting the rebellious Irish, and a bulwark against the Spanish Armada.

In 1796 during the French Wars, Bantry Bay was the scene of a day-long battle between a British fleet of eighteen warships and an invading fleet numbering twenty-four vessels. From 10a.m. until 5.00p.m. gun smoke was thick over the Bay as the French ships came to close quarters with the British. Many British ships were damaged but the Frenchmen headed for home and there is no record of their losses. In 1798 there was yet another French incursion into Bantry Bay, but this too was unsuccessful. The effect of these invasion attempts caused fortifications to be built along certain river estuaries, including Bantry Bay. The defences for the latter consisted of four Martello towers, a redoubt, and a signal tower on Bere Island with similar defences on the smaller islands. All were completed by 1807.

From 1860 onwards the defences on Bere Island were allowed to disappear, even though there was a military recommendation stating clearly that these needed to be maintained. Nevertheless, in 1884 the Defence Committee had decided to give up its lease on the lands occupied by the fortifications. It took until 1889 and a strongly worded letter from Rear Admiral Tryon to the Director of Artillery, to cause a joint Royal Engineers and Royal Artillery Works Committee to take action. This organisation had been set up in 1885 and was responsible to the Defence Committee, which instructed it to take a hard look at what Tryon considered to be the strategic defences necessary for both Berehaven and Lough Swilly. His letter and the response to it ran as follows:

Rear-Admiral Sir George Tryon, K.C.B.,
to Major-General H.J. Alderson, C.B., Director of Artillery.

Admiralty, Spring Gardens. 6 February, 1889.

My dear Alderson,

With reference to our chat yesterday afternoon, my point is this: while we are providing some defensive works and talk of providing more for certain ports, and those defences which may secure the safety of that which is within them, they do nothing towards assisting us in providing the safe passage of vessels carrying that which is vital to our existence – food.

This is a new feature, or, at all events, it did not press so heavily during our last great wars, and the point I named with reference to affording assistance by means of a defended harbour, well placed for mercantile strategic purposes, has, I believe, escaped attention, and, indeed, it is to a very considerable extent new and due to steam propulsion, which will enable vessels to derive full advantage from one. If you look at the lines of trade and commerce on a chart, you will appreciate at once how easy it is to interrupt them, how congested the lines become here and there, how great are the facilities offered to an enemy to interfere with them, and how difficult it is to defend then.

Now, with map in mind's eye, consider Lough Swilly and Berehaven to be defended ports, one in the N.W. and another in the S.W. of Ireland, on the very verge of the wide ocean, and I think you will come to the conclusion that nature has provided us with two ports, admirably adapted to welcome coming and to speed parting friends. When a vessel has attained either of those ports, with the aid of our telegraph and signal stations, we should be able to pass her, at all events, from port to port, and if chased, she would have the choice of defended ports on either side to make for – Queenstown, Milford, Plymouth, or Bristol Channel, a cul-de-sac, up which an up enemy would be rash to enter unless he was fully acquainted as to the position of our ships. The passage of American trade north of Ireland would be greatly facilitated by providing a defended port at Lough Swilly. The Mersey and the Clyde are entered at high water; vessels in Irish ports would be able to time their arrival to save the tide. Conditions due to modern warfare, as well as the urgent requirements of the country, cause me to advocate the taking advantage of positions nature has provided to our hands, and those conditions and requirements have only become prominent of late years, and I do not consider it is a subject that should he burked, or, at all events, not thought out.

I am, etc.
G. TRYON
(If it commends itself to you pray advocate it.)

The reply, included in a report, ran as follows:

The Royal Artillery and Royal Engineers Works Committee have considered Sir G. Tryon's letter … and submit the following remarks:

Lord Morley's Committee did not discountenance the idea of defending places of secondary importunce, but refrained from recommending works at such places as the Shannon, Loughs Foyle and Swilly, because they were impressed with the necessity of rendering the larger mercantile ports as far as possible secure from attack before making any attempt to protect places of secondary importance.

The Defence Committee recommended works at Lough Foyle, which have not yet been carried out. They also recommended that the defences of Lough Swilly should be dismantled.

The Committee would point out that in all previous considerations of this subject the question has only been approached from the point of view of denying these harbours to an enemy's cruisers, not with the object of affording a secure refuge to our own men-of-war and to the vessels of our mercantile marine. This point appears to be raised for the first time by Sir G. Tryon's letter referred to above.

The Committee agree with Sir G. Tryon that one defended harbour in the north-west and one in the south-west of Ireland would be of great value to our mercantile marine in the event of war with a maritime Power, and they are of opinion that, as regards the former, Lough Swilly is in every way to be preferred to Lough Foyle; the navigation is simpler, the anchorage more roomy, and it is more easily defended.

As regards the defended harbour in the south-west of Ireland, they consider Berehaven (Bantry Bay) to be the most suitable, lying as it does very near the track of homeward-bound vessels, being easy of access, affording good anchorage, and capable of being easily defended.

H. L. GEARY, Colonel, R.A.,
President, R.A. and R.E. Works Committee.
18 April 1889.

Having examined the situation at the Lough Swilly forts, the committee turned its attention southwards to Berehaven. It considered that it was vital to defend both entrances and to secure an effective command of the entire harbour, including as much as possible of Bantry Bay. The members examined the four Martello Towers and considered these commanding sites as suitable for more formidable defence constructions. At the narrow western end of the anchorage there was an existing fort and the committee could find no better place for rearmament with guns ranging from 6-inch cannon down to light 3-pounders. This old fort would have to be adapted to take these guns and a new road would be needed.

The other types of guns proposed for Berehaven were not very different from the list recommended for Lough Swilly, but greater numbers were recommended: the island might be exposed to much heavier attacks than the latter because shorter ranges would be involved. The Committee considered that the guns proposed for both the southern and northern forts would meet minimum requirements.

In the late nineteenth century a thorough military survey was undertaken and in 1894 the government acquired parcels of land by Compulsory Purchase Order. Rather cynically, one feels, this order was issued on St Patrick's Day and many islanders were displaced – however the families in these sections were rehoused. Red lines on the map indicated land fenced off by the army: one line on the east ran north–south along the west border of Rerrin, cutting it and Ardaragh east and west off from the rest of the island. A second north–south red line on the west cut off a section of Derrycreeveen. Henceforth islanders referred to locations as being 'east or west of the red line'.

Work on fortifications and associated buildings was begun by the Royal Engineers, assisted by civilian contractors. A dredger and a barge supplied sand for mortar and concrete – though sea sand is not the best ingredient for these mixes. A coastguard station at Lawrence's Cove, the main harbour, was completed and this was followed by

Taken at Bere Island in 1900. Sailors and gunners unload the barrel of a 9.2-inch gun in St Lawrence Cove, prior to taking it to its position on a special trolley.

Derrycreeveen Barracks. By 1903 Ardnakinna Barracks, Rerrin Battery, Rerrin Redoubt, and Reenduff Battery were completed. In 1904 another barracks was built at Laurence's Cove and later Lonehort Battery was established. A beacon required by the coastguard was built at Ardnakinna in 1912.

At the time when this formidable array of defences had begun, the mainland was surveyed because it offered a back door possibility to potential European enemies. The survey was undertaken by a Lt-Col. C.H. Pickwood, an experienced artillery officer, who recorded his findings in a diary as he closely studied a lengthy stretch of the coast and a wide swathe of its hinterland. He was looking for places where an enemy could bring guns ashore and position them to reduce the proposed improved island defences. The following extracts from his diary show, '4th February: Left Cork by the 11.35a.m. train for Kenmare. Stayed at Southern Hotel, extremely comfortable first-class hotel. Weather very wet and misty.'

And on the following day:

Hired car, drove to Kilmakilloge (16 miles) beautiful and good road fit for
bicycle which could be hired in Kenmare. Hired a poor but clean bed at
James Sullivan's, 'The Master' public house. Difficulty about food which
should be taken with one on this road. Excellent bread, milk and eggs pro-
curable, but nothing else. Passed Lehid Harbour on the way but returned
there at 2.00p.m. to examine it at low water. Entrance very shallow and
rocky; one landing place possible for field guns at all times in good weather,
other landing places at high water. Examined all the roads around Lehid
and walked to a place above Kilmakilloge by another road. The latter place
has a harbour with a waterway of 7 to 17 feet according to tide – there is a
good stone wharf 150 yards long and 20 feet wide at the eastern end of it.
Field-guns and others, up to perhaps 2½ tons in weight, could easily be
landed in places without the aid of sheers …

Another day:

In the afternoon drove 8 miles in the direction of the mountains overlooking Berehaven. The road ends abruptly against the face of a hill where a
footpath only is to be seen. So field-gun mounted on its carriage could be
dragged up. The ascent is over a sort of 'col' for about 500 feet, then a fall
and a rise later to a height of about 1600 feet. Arrived at Ardgroom Village,
9 miles, at dusk – great difficulty in getting a lodging – found poor but
comfortable quarters in a draper's shop, people named Sullivan – road to
Ardgroom good and hard. Two rather long but not steep ascents on the
way. Examined the southern and western shores of the harbour. Landing of
field and light siege-guns could be made at various places.

On the fourth day the colonel wrote:

On the Kenmare River coast. [Incidentally, the Kenmare River is a misno-

mer; it is actually a deep inlet of the sea]. At 1p.m. I drove to south eastern
end of Glenbeg Lake and walked to the mountain and climbed it to about
1200 feet. Bringing guns up the valley below to the high grounds is out
of the question. From this spot and the top of Maulin (500 feet higher)
Berehaven Harbour, most of Bere Island and its Western Defences can be
seen, distance 700 yards. It is to be remembered that the mountain is 2,000
feet high and is covered with wet bog. My guide was a gamekeeper who
knew the mountain well, but a youth who accompanied us was unable to
continue and went back when half-way up. The approaches to the high
ground overlooking Berehaven Harbour and its defences are therefore not
being thought of for Artillery, or, I should say, any men but mountaineers.

On the fifth day the officer noted:

The bay called Ballycrovane is open and fairly well sheltered – big vessels
could anchor in it. Luggers of 40 tons enter Ballycrovane Harbour which is
rocky, but which has a pier. Field and light siege-guns could be landed on
the main road. There is a fine open sandy beach here and a number of guns,
horses and men could rapidly be landed in fair weather close to the main
road.

Using all forms of transport, including his sturdy legs, the officer's
investigations were much more intensive than these extracts indicate.
Lt-Col. Pickwood wrote of his final day:

During my visit all possible approaches by road from the Kenmare River
to Berehaven were examined by me on foot where necessary. This entailed
a great deal of walking and it is certain that for practical purposes by an
attacking force in winter, and most probably always, almost all but the
main road round the Bere Peninsula may be omitted from consideration.
In the summertime the bog is a little more dry, I am told, but not much so.
The main road is hard, dry, and good always.

And along this road the redoubtable Pickwood marched onwards … and into the pages of history. Right up until the forts were handed back in 1938 Britain was acutely aware of the dangers that the hinterland of each fort could present. In Ireland one field gun properly positioned and manned by foreign enemies or local dissidents could reduce coastal defences to rubble. When the Emergency began, the Irish Army deployed mobile forces to guard against back-door invaders.

After the colonel's survey and the construction work, gunners from the Royal Garrison Artillery at Spike were transferred to the island to land several large guns and many lesser ones from Woolwich Arsenal. Eventually, four large guns had been positioned, together with a greater one weighing 27 tons while a similar heavyweight was waiting to be installed. By 1911 there was a total of nineteen guns in position. A local newspaper expected that Bere Island, 'would be the most strongly fortified place for its extent in the British Isles'. The large-scale works required back-up in terms of married quarters at both ends of the island, and these were built to the design of those in Singapore. The installation of an electricity supply, solely for army use, provided power for the searchlights which swept the channel and the open sea. A water supply was pumped into the army houses and barracks and the government acquired more land for a rifle range.

The guns on the island were regularly fired during 'practice shoots' and for calibration. When this happened the islanders had to evacuate their homes and on one occasion, a complete ceiling collapsed from the blast. The guns at the west end of the island were intended for 'hostilities only'. Designed to counter enemies who had broached the mainland harbour, they could never be tested in peacetime as they were unable to swivel out to sea. Naval exercises took place to test the effectiveness of the coastal defences and a large hole, still to be seen in a cliff, was the result of a misdirected shell fired from a warship out in Bantry Bay.

In the Berehaven anchorage there were constant visits from the Channel Fleet, the Home Fleet, or the Atlantic Fleet; these took it in turns for a few weeks each summer during exercises. A local journalist wrote, 'The peace of the island is being disturbed by warships entering the harbour. The line of ships extends for miles but they close up when they drop anchor and the island's population is increased by about 13,000 men.' In 1906 the anchorage was black with ships from shore to shore and as local people said, 'One could walk to the mainland from Bere Island simply by stepping from ship to ship.' At the weekend, concerts were held on various ships and the local inhabitants would stand outside their homes and listen as the music wafted on the evening air and, in addition to this pleasure, of course the local economy benefited as well.

Chapter 5

The Guardians of Lough Swilly

Donegal, the most northerly county of the island of Ireland, notable for its picturesque rugged scenery, was the last outpost of the old Gaelic order, which ended after the disastrous Battle of Kinsale in 1601. After the battle, the chiefs of the O'Donnell clan, together with their allies the O'Neills of Tyrone, were surrounded by enemies and the spies of James I. Forced into exile, they sailed in 1607 from the wide deep anchorage of Lough Swilly to the continent, in an episode known as The Flight of the Earls. The lough that facilitated their departure pierces Donegal's northern coast like a fjord, and is navigable for about twenty-five miles south to the town of Letterkenny.

About 2,600 years ago the Celts, who knew how to make iron, came here and left traces of their metal industry and also the remains of a circular earthen fort. Less industrious warriors followed and the area was raided by Vikings and Danes in the ninth century. Eventually they were defeated by the local chieftain in AD 833, whose son laid waste to their settlements – the remains of these are still evident.

On the lough's eastern shore near its entrance, Dunree Head stands

The entrance to Fort Dunree with the original old fort, now a museum, on the left.

One of the pair of 9.2 inch guns of Fort Lenan in 1940.

335ft at the top of a small rocky peninsula. For centuries a fort has stood here, its name being interpreted in many ways, including The King's Fort or The Heather Fort. Various earthen forts were built on both shores and eventually these numbered seven: Dunree, Ned's Point, Salt Pan Battery at Buncrana, Down Fort on Inch Island, Rathmullen, Knockalla, and Machamish (see colour section).

By the end of the eighteenth century there were hopes of a French invasion to assist the United Irishmen in their struggle for freedom. When a French squadron was *en route* to land troops in Co. Mayo it encountered a British fleet and one of the most significant sea battles in Irish history ensued. The French flagship *Hoche*, having fought bravely for over three hours, was finally captured and towed into Lough Swilly. The prisoners landed on its shore included the United Ireland leader, Wolfe Tone. This attempted invasion, and two similar French forays into Bantry Bay, caused Britain to build more substantial fortifications to protect these strategic anchorages. By 1800 some of the Lough Swilly forts were made redundant because improvements in artillery meant that the entire lough could now be covered by guns sited in fewer forts.

The Napoleonic Wars caused Fort Dunree to be transformed by Sir William Augustus Smith, an infantry militia captain who was deeply involved in the lough's defences, though he had no formal engineering qualifications. His sketches and drawings, which can be seen in the Library of Trinity College, Dublin, show several buildings, a perimeter wall, a lower battery and a circular gun emplacement on the highest point of Dunree Head. A Martello tower was added and the whole edifice was described in 1812 as 'an artillery station garrisoned by a master gunner and 27 men'.

The Crimean War in the 1850s brought continued improvements in gunnery which called for extra manning levels. With the emphasis on local men to garrison these stations, militias were now formed. The army's Adjutant General saw this as an opportunity to save

A close view of the pair of 6-inch guns positioned near the top of Dunree Hill.

money by suggesting that Fort Dunree be manned only in an emergency. However, higher authority would not accept this because of the undoubted strategic value of the Lough in ensuring safe passage on the North Atlantic. These changes caused Fort Dunree to be remodelled in 1884, equipping it with the latest 4.7-inch guns. Concurrently, the naval value of Lough Swilly was the subject of careful scrutiny by a joint Army–Navy board which was provoked by the Tryon Report mentioned earlier in regard to Berehaven.

Afterwards, great advances in warship design and the consequent effect on coast defences by the turn of the new century caused the formation of a joint Royal Artillery–Royal Engineers Works Committee (this was to be the first of many). This initial body believed that:

The mighty barrel of one of Fort Lenan's 9.2-inch long-range guns.

It is necessary to bring the navigable channel under fire throughout the whole of this length, inasmuch as the channel is free from obstruction, and vessels entering at high speed might run past the defences, if they could count upon gaining undefended water beyond. It is also to be borne in mind that there is no perfectly sheltered harbour, short of Rathmullen Roadstead, 12 miles from the entrance. The object of the defences should be: first, to command the entrance to the Lough, with the double aims of denying the shelter of the headlands to an enemy, and of giving the earliest protection to pursue vessels seeking to enter; secondly, to command the inner waters to such an extent that no enemy could run past the defences, or remain unmolested in any part of the Lough.

At the time, the British Empire seemed invincible. Nevertheless, in a tiny corner of its vast domain its masters saw a chink in its armour and they decided to further reinforce the defences of Lough Swilly. Five miles nearer to the mouth of the lough from Dunree it was decided to build a modern state-of-the-art fortification on Lenan Hill.

Work started in 1901 and the new fort was operational by the following year. It was sited on a cliff facing seawards and it had three concrete gun positions backed up by magazines, stores, barracks and a guardhouse.

The gun positions mounted heavy 9.2-inch guns which were served by magazines beneath them and these guns were linked by sunken roads radiating from the centre of the fort. Thus the gunners would be protected as they ran to their action stations. Overlooking the batteries stood the commander's observation post and behind this were two sunken positions called cells. These housed Position Finders essential for long-range gunnery which was beyond the capability of DRFs. Protected by a wide and deep ditch on its landward side with a drawbridge to gain entrance, the complete installation was enclosed by a barbed wire fence. It had cost £25,000, a sizeable sum at the beginning of the twentieth century.

The garrison in the new fort was limited to twenty-eight all ranks but there was provision for two dozen more to be housed in wartime conditions. At this time there were three forts on the eastern side of the lough but the fort at Ned's Point was relegated to a practice installation. A Belfast District Defence Scheme, which took in the whole of the Inishowen Peninsula, had been updated on 1 January 1904; its authors believed that the principal danger to Lough Swilly would come from an onslaught by several armoured cruisers and torpedo boats.

The posturing of his Germanic Majesty Emperor Wilhelm II, posed a growing threat to Britain's command of the sea and an arms race between the two nations accelerated and inexorably led to the worldwide conflagration, the Great War. Yet another joint Admiralty–Army committee was set up with a limited remit covering only those major naval bases which were considered likely to be attacked by capital ships. None of the Irish bases were in this category, and the only effect on Lough Swilly was the removal of one of the heavy guns, which was

The layout of Fort Dunree is clearly seen in this aerial photograph. At the top are the emplacements for the two 6-inch guns, while at the bottom right sits the original fort which now houses a splendid museum.

proving troublesome and was dismounted.

With the outbreak of the Great War in 1914 the landward defence of Fort Dunree had to be considered because of the uneasy political situation in Ireland. There was a danger of attacks by 'disaffected local people' brought on by the latest postponement of Irish Home Rule which had dragged on for over fifty years. To increase protection on the landward side of Dunree a number of concrete blockhouses were erected and the existing perimeter fence was heavily laced with barbed wire – though none was tested.

Chapter 6

The Development of Coast Artillery

There had been very little change in the basic concept of the cannon from 1750 until 1880. By that year, the standard gun for coastal forts was a smooth bore gun which weighed about 2½ tons and could despatch a cannonball weighing 24lbs. After a further thirty years this weapon was superseded by a 32-pounder which weighed about 2.8 tons, though there was very little improvement in the maximum range of guns until the 60-pounder arrived.

A cannon, cast in metal, had to be loaded from its muzzle; first the gunpowder would be poured down the barrel, followed by a wad, all consolidated by vigorous tamping. Next, the cannonball, which could weigh up to 60lbs or more, would be rolled down and rammed tightly against the wad. This cumbersome operation was carried out without protection for the gun crew who were often in the face of the enemy. The loaders then retired and, after sighting the weapon, the gun-layers discharged it by applying a glowing taper to the touch-hole. The whole procedure was dangerous and time-consuming and if the cannon was overcharged, or there was a fault in its casting, the weapon could explode and wipe out the crew. In the early 1850s, the idea of 'rifling' or

An 'exploded view' of the components of a typical seventeenth-century cannon. The spigots of the barrel are held down by metal cleats onto the timber carriage. On the left is a timber wedge for elevating the barrel, with, on the right, a ramming and clearing rod.

cutting grooves in the smooth barrel of a muzzle-loader was conceived; these would cause projectiles to spin in flight and keep to their correct line.

As guns became more powerful, controlling the burning rate of gunpowder charges, and the explosion this unleashed, required massive strength in the weapon. Thus the guns grew huge at one end with comparatively short barrels and a rather dumpy profile emerged. Now various forms of high-explosives replaced gunpowder, which had originated in ancient China.

In Britain, William Armstrong designed a new type of weapon which was much lighter and stronger. To simplify loading, Armstrong adopted a large door, called the breech block, which was fitted to where the touchhole previously had been and thereby eliminated the cumbersome and dangerous procedure of muzzle-loading. Armstrong's method was taken up by the Royal Navy, which soon found out that the new guns were no quicker to operate than the old ones and, in fact, were less effective at piercing the armour that now clad most naval vessels. This was

Laying a muzzle-loading cannon. The gun is mounted on an inclined carriage which helps to dampen the recoil when the weapon is fired. Here the chief gunner is sighting the weapon while his crew use wooden staves to traverse the wheels of the carriage on an iron ring.

sufficiently serious to cause the Navy to revert to muzzle-loaders, albeit now rifled. However, breech-loading was much quicker and easier and eventually this method prevailed.

Ammunition became a two-piece package as propellant now came in bagged cartridges to fire a separate shell. After firing, the barrel had to be swabbed out with water to clear burning embers from the bag which could cause a disastrous premature explosion on reloading. Continuous heavy firing at full charge wore out the rifling of the barrel which had a working life of about 450 rounds at maximum charge. After that the barrel had to be relined and mountings were strengthened in later designs.

Many of the cannon equipping the Irish forts in the early nineteenth century were mounted on a disappearing carriage. This photograph shows one such gun in the firing position. Afterwards it would be retracted below the protection of a parapet where it could be reloaded by its crew who would now be protected from hostile fire, a major improvement for muzzle-loaders.

In 1879 Krupp in Germany developed a 24cm gun, and the British Admiralty called for a similar weapon and thus the 9.2-inch emerged, which culminated in the Mk X which came into service in 1900. This became Britain's most powerful coastal defence weapon and it soon equipped most of the defences of the United Kingdom which, of course, included Ireland. It could fire a 330lb shell to a range of 25,700 yards and at shorter distances, this shell could penetrate 14 inches of armour plate.

The gun's mounting took the form of a high pedestal which allowed the gun to clear a 6ft 6ins parapet. A circular steel platform formed a walkway around the gun and shielded personnel in the shell-pit underneath. Here there were trolleys running on rails which deliv-

The development of coast defence guns culminated with the 9.2-inch weapon circa 1900. Apart from some refinements this remained in service right up to the end of the Second World War. As can be seen, there was a lot of mechanical hardware underneath the actual gun.

ered ammunition to the gunners above by means of hydraulic lifts. The 9.2-inch gun was described as a counter-bombardment weapon, a description which told an attacker that he would get as good as he dished out.

From 1888 a new gun of slightly lesser calibre, at 6 inches, was introduced and became a standard weapon in its own right. It could take on warships as powerful as cruisers, and it did just that as described in a later chapter. In some forts it was the sole equipment and in others it was used to bolster the larger 9.2-inch weapon. It had five different mountings, virtually all of which were simple pedestals.

In 1898 a highly efficient single-motion breech was introduced which speeded up loading and firing, and the range was increased from 11,800 to 16,500 yards. Manned by an experienced crew, it could deliver eight rounds per minute. Incidentally, its gun pit was open at the back to allow enemy shells an escape route if they didn't explode on first contact – an event which was quite common in early times. The 6-inch gun remained in service in coastal forts until the end of the 1950s when coastal defence artillery in fixed positions, which had endured for 400 years, was abandoned.

Chapter 7

The Great War

By the beginning of the twentieth century the two forts in Donegal, Dunree and Lenan, were the main points of defence at Lough Swilly. The anchorage became busier with frequent naval visits and manoeuvres and the presence of a permanent guardship stationed at Rathmullen. Further improvements continued, including a practice battery and a tennis court at Dunree. By 1911 there were forty all ranks there and twenty-eight in Lenan, which was well below the capacity of this new fort. From 1912 the gunners carried out live firing practices each year, using a brace of the latest 6-inch guns on the top of Dunree Head where they are still preserved.

Soon the forts were put on a war footing. The deep anchorage now became an ideal collection point where merchantmen would gather to form into transatlantic convoys before setting out on their perilous voyages. In October 1916 the Grand Fleet arrived from its base at Scapa Flow in Scotland where it was reckoned to be vulnerable to the U-boats of the Imperial German Navy. Admiral Lord Jellicoe declared, 'For the first time since the declaration of war the fleet occupied a secure base.' In addition to capital ships and destroyers there were minesweepers, tankers, store and repair ships, giving a total of forty vessels. Even here there were dangers along this coast. A tremendous explosion out at sea was heard in the forts; it signalled that HMS *Audacious* had been sunk, and the next day upturned lifeboats were floating in the lough.

These stirring events were witnessed by Denis Ireland, a well-known author between the wars. He was stationed at Fort Dunree, as an infantry subaltern whose regiment was billeted under canvas there before being despatched to the Western Front. One morning he and his comrades awoke and were astonished to see the whole of the Grand Fleet at anchor in the roadstead off Rathmullen. He described the activity that followed:

> Anti-submarine nets are laid across the narrows below the fort; the crews are landed and marched around the countryside; and bum-boat men from Buncrana and Rathmullen do a roaring trade in fresh vegetables and rabbits. Then fog descends and the Grand Fleet is blotted from our sight.

This gave the writer an opportunity to visit his brother who was the navigating officer on HMS *Birmingham*. He recalled:

> After two days, while the fog continued, the fleet remained invisible in the Lough. Then the fog lifted and the fleet departed during the night, filing in procession through the narrows under the glare of searchlights from the forts. By the light of his binnacle I could see my brother standing at the wheel and as it turned out this was the last-but-one time when I saw him alive. The whole spectacle provided me with a strange experience. What exactly happened cannot be put into words; for a moment the curtain of time seemed to be drawn back and I was conscious of the events of two centuries unrolling themselves simultaneously as if the old philosophical idea of the point at which, but for the illusion of the curtain which is called 'time', the past, the present, and the future co-exist, had been demonstrated before my eyes like a laboratory experiment in physics.

This drawing shows a lone sentry guarding the guns of a remote coastal fort as the year 1915 dawns.

I remember that I stood on the cliffs beside the fort, staring through my binoculars at the point where the tail end of the fleet was on the point of disappearing into the darkness at the mouth of Lough Swilly against the background of the cliffs of Fanad, when suddenly there was an uncanny white light on the water, and what can only be described as a mimic sea-fight, a silent manoeuvring without the sound of guns. A ghostly frigate seemed to be sailing through the files of the Grand Fleet; in the uncanny white light on the sea I was watching a terrible battle, the tension so colossal that it took upon itself the dimensions of a collision between principalities and powers. Then the white light faded, the tension relaxed, the ghostly battle was over, and I was left standing on the cliffs staring at the spot where the last ships of the Grand Fleet had disappeared in the darkness, wondering if I had seen, what I had seen.

For years I spoke to no one about it, since the thing seemed incapable of explanation. Then, I began to read the history of my country for the first time, since, like all good Protestant Ulstermen, I had been brought up to believe that Irish history consisted of nothing but cattle raids. And reading this history I discovered that the point over which I had seen the Grand Fleet disappearing into the darkness in October 1916 was the exact point where, in October 1798, a fierce sea battle had been fought. The French frigate *Hoche*, bearing Wolfe Tone as a passenger, had defended herself for 6 hours under the fire of an entire English squadron, so that the ghostly battle I had seen had been a flashback from the eighteenth century into the twentieth century. In the jargon of science, the simultaneous imposition upon the screen of my consciousness of two apparently time-separated events.

The 1798 battle had been real enough and the *Hoche* had been beached on the shores of the lough. Wolfe Tone and other prisoners were put ashore; the United Irishman, after years of neglect, is recognised as a great patriot and his death is commemorated annually. The guns from the *Hoche* were installed in the Lough Swilly forts and served there for many years.

Denis Ireland and his men departed for the front; security was further tightened and the forts buzzed with activity and the lough was further enlivened by continuous comings and goings. When unidentified vessels were spotted, the garrison stood to in rifle pits around the guns, ready for instant action. When floating mines appeared they were dramatically disarmed: riflemen enjoyed exploding them and great spouts erupted from the water as the marksmen proved that they could hit the protruding detonator horns. Flashing lights were seen on the Fanad Mountains where a suspected spy was lurking but efforts to catch him were unavailing. The alarm was sounded many times, even when a flock of wild geese was passing over giving the appearance of an air raid.

All the while the forts were being improved by tradesmen earning £5 per week, high pay indeed for those times. To keep up morale a band played on the green, and recruits engaged in rifle and machine-gun practice before a medical to see if they were fit enough to be sent to the Western Front. Three rowing boats were provided from which the garrison and the transient troops enjoyed the more peaceful pastime of angling. As the Great War progressed the danger of German surface vessels disappeared, although the U-boats were still a menace, and many gunners were taken away from their duties and despatched to the Western Front. With the return of peace, activity at Lough Swilly diminished and signs of quieter times reappeared. Nature gradually reclaimed the road which ran between the two forts, and the grass and the streams came back.

Meanwhile, down in the south there was a reduction in the number of large warships visiting Berehaven. These Leviathans had taken up their wartime stations but would occasionally reappear for maintenance. During this work these powerful warships were helpless once their boilers were extinguished as all their guns, winches and machinery were steam-operated. Since it took forty-eight hours to get up steam, they were extremely vulnerable and required elaborate protection. Berehaven buzzed with activity generated by destroyers, sloops, torpedo boats and armed trawlers as they came and went on escort duty and patrols to combat U-boats. The arrival in 1917 of the US destroyers, submarines, and maritime aircraft improved matters and all the Cork bases then began to prove their worth.

On Bere Island, the outbreak of war called for many modifications to earlier defence plans and by the end of the conflict it boasted a total of a dozen guns, mainly of 6-inch calibre, distributed to three batteries at each of the entrances to the haven. The island became a last staging post before troops were sent off to France, similar to the arrangement at Lough Swilly. To take this influx, huts were constructed on many sites and a barracks was built in Lonehort, together with a military hospital. The latter was needed for the steady stream of wounded soldiers who were brought there to recuperate before being either demobbed or sent back again to the Front, depending on the severity of their wounds. Five thousand men of the Connaught Rangers passed through Bere Island but only a fraction of them returned. The Great War was supposed to be 'the war to end all wars' – a pious hope indeed.

Chapter 8

Bombardment

Boom, crash! Boom, crash! The deafening noise of heavy naval guns as they sent their shells screaming through a misty December morning in 1914 as the Great War gathered momentum. A squadron of battle cruisers was bombarding shore defences in a raid to damage port facilities and create alarm among the civilian population. The attack could have been the forerunner of an invasion.

The first warship opened fire on the shore batteries with her 11-inch guns and at 0800 hours the first round crashed ashore. It was spot-on for range and fell between two batteries, killing four soldiers. At first, the gunners in the coastal defence batteries mistook the warships for their own but, very quickly, manned the guns. To the sound of terrifying crashes, shells slammed into the houses just behind the shoreline. A heavy cruiser was now engaged by the shore batteries at a range of 600 yards and though the first ranging shells fell short, the third round was a hit and carried away a good part of the vessel's bridge, disabling two of its 5.9-inch guns and detonating deck ammunition which killed nine seamen.

Now the three enemy ships discharged a simultaneous broadside which rained down on another shore battery. As the ground shook around them, stretcher-bearers raced to the wounded. They saw that the battery itself was unscathed, but the houses behind it had taken a severe battering. Soon shells from another salvo arrived, sweeping away both wounded and their would-be rescuers. An orange glow flared in the sky adding to the scene of death and destruction.

Earlier, a reserve officer, a doctor, alerted by the gunfire and knowing that there were no firing practices that morning, donned his uniform, grabbed his bike, and made his way to the shore defences as quickly as possible. It was difficult to get through townsfolk milling around in the streets, some excited by the noise and racing towards the promenade for a better view, others intent at getting as far away as possible. The most obvious damage was to the town's gas-holder which caused a blaze which could be seen for miles. Industry suffered as workshops and plant were destroyed and timber stocks went up in smoke. But the worst damage was to houses, whose occupants were killed and injured – though there were some miraculous escapes.

A factory worker described the attack:

> When we were told about the enemy ships we thought it was a joke, but no sooner had the messenger left us that we heard a rumbling noise which gradually grew louder. We realised it was gunfire and we could hear the shells passing overhead. On reaching the street, everybody was making for home, but we ran towards the seafront and plainly saw one of the ships firing broadsides in our direction. It was certainly time to seek shelter.

All the time the shore batteries continued firing, concentrating their aim on the upper works of the ships because their 6-inch shells were seen to be bouncing off their armoured hulls. Eventually, the naval squadron, harassed all the time by the coastal guns, disappeared into the mist pursued by continuous fire until the intruders were virtually six miles away. In the forty-two minutes of the engagement, the defenders had fired 123 rounds. Between the gunners and civilians, 114 people had lost their lives.

This bombardment was the first time that the coastal forts of the British Isles had seen action and it demonstrated how an attack by sea raiders would dramatically wreak death and destruction. The foregoing is not a film scenario, it is a report of what actually happened when German cruisers bombarded Hartlepool on the north-east coast of England. The carnage could well have been replicated in Ireland in either World Wars; had Cork's harbour defences been penetrated by enemy vessels the devastation can only be imagined.

In the Hartlepool attack, two of the German battle cruisers were of the latest type and very well armed with ten 11-inch guns, supplemented by a dozen 5.9-inch weapons; even the less modern vessel of the trio had a dozen 8.2-inch guns. The British gunners depended on their standard 6-inch guns; had these been supplemented by 9.2-inch weapons, and had the enemy been identified earlier, the German ships would not have escaped with minor damage.

Immediately before the Second World War broke out, Winston Churchill made the following comment:

> The progress in RDF (Radar), especially applied to range-finding, must surely be of high consequence to the Navy. It would give power to engage an enemy, irrespective of visibility. How different would have been the fate of the German battle cruisers when they attacked Hartlepool in 1914 if we could have pierced the mist then.

Radar stations had been set up along the south and east coasts of the UK a couple of years before the hand back of the Irish forts, but this innovation was still on the secret list and was never available to the Irish gunners, assuming it had been possible to adopt it. Radar transformed the use of coastal guns; not only could target vessels be clearly tracked but the fall of shot could also be seen and quick corrections made, while at night-time it lifted the cloak of darkness.

Chapter 9

The Anglo-Irish Treaty

On the outbreak of the Great War the British Government put the long-discussed question of Home Rule on the long finger once more. This caused a split in the Irish Volunteers; William Redmond MP called upon them and others to go out and fight, not for a free Ireland, but for 'poor little Catholic Belgium now being trampled by the German hordes'. Those who agreed with him were now called the Irish National Volunteers. The remainder of the Irish Volunteers, who were not lulled into this somewhat false invitation, stayed at home and despite the confusion caused by countermanding orders, in 1916 they fought for an Irish Republic. At the end of week-long hostilities, mainly in Dublin, the Volunteers surrendered and sixteen of their leaders were executed.

When the survivors were released from prison, the fight for freedom continued and the Volunteers, now generally known as the Irish Republican Army, gradually continued the armed struggle which was to become a bloody conflict in 1920 until the summer of 1921 when a truce was concluded. This led to negotiations and a Treaty was signed in December 1921. The terms of this were not agreeable to a percentage of the Irish electorate. The status of Ireland was given in Article No. 1:

Cork City Barracks. 1922. A British detachment leaves with its pack mules.

Ireland shall have the constitutional status in the Community of Nations known as the British Empire as the Dominion of Canada, the Commonwealth of Australia, the Dominion of New Zealand, and the Union of South Africa, with a Parliament having powers to make laws for the peace order and good government of Ireland and an Executive responsible to that Parliament and shall be styled and known as the Irish Free State.

The terms of the Treaty included the following Annex which detailed the British demand for naval facilities in Ireland. Michael Collins agreed to these requirements saying, 'Of course, you must have the ports.' Unusually, de Valera agreed with him in his Document No. 2, which he put forward to replace the Treaty.

The Annex, known as Article 6 and 7, was as follows:

6. Until an arrangement has been made between the British and Irish Governments whereby the Irish Free State undertakes her own coastal defence, the defence by sea of Great Britain and Ireland shall be undertaken by His Majesty's Imperial Forces, but this shall not prevent the construction

Cork City Barracks, 1922. Careless of the protocol which decrees that the national flag must never touch the ground, British troops haul down the Union Jack for the last time.

or maintenance by the Government of the Irish Free State of such vessels as are necessary for the protection of the Revenue or the Fisheries.

The foregoing provisions of this article shall be reviewed at a conference of Representatives of the British and Irish Governments to be held at the expiration of five years from the date hereof with a view to the undertaking by Ireland of a share in her own coastal defence.

7. The Government of the Irish Free State shall afford to His Majesty's Imperial Forces:

(a) In time of peace such harbour and other facilities as are indicated in the Annex hereto, or such other facilities as may from time to time be agreed between the British Government and the Government of the Irish Free State; and

(b) In time of war or strained relations with a Foreign Power such harbour and other facilities as the British Government may require for the purposes of such defence as aforesaid.

1. The following are the specific facilities required:

Dockyard Port at Berehaven
(a) Admiralty property and rights to be retained as at the date hereof. Harbour defences to remain in charge of British care and maintenance parties.
Queenstown
(b) Harbour defences to remain in charge of British care and maintenance parties. Certain mooring buoys to be retained for use of His Majesty's ships.
Belfast Lough
(c) Harbour defences to remain in charge of British care and maintenance parties. [This was a cynical gesture on the part of the British who had already copper-fastened this area by the Government of Ireland Act in 1920, and knew that the futile 'Boundary Commission' would never include Belfast Lough in the Free State.]
Lough Swilly
(d) Harbour defences to remain in charge of British care and maintenance parties.
Aviation
(e) Facilities in the neighbourhood of the above ports for coastal defence by air.
Oil Fuel Storage
(f) To be offered for sale to commercial companies under guarantee that purchasers shall maintain a certain minimum stock for Admiralty purposes at Haulbowline and Rathmullen.

After it was signed, reactions to the Treaty were predictable. Speaking in the House of Commons, Winston Churchill declared:

As to the Navy, nothing has been conceded that was essential to the security of Great Britain. It is true that in five years there might be a conference on the subject. That is quite reasonable. We might wish to ask for other facilities than those now given. It is conceivable that in five years time the Irish Government may be very glad to see our Navy bringing custom into Irish ports, when some of the present bitterness has passed away. It is also possible that in ten or twenty years time our government and the Admiralty might be willing to allow the Irish Free State to construct motor-boats and so forth for hunting submarines, whilst at the same time refusing the right to construct submarines and mine-layers or other craft which might be a source of injury to this country. These matters are entirely under the control of the Imperial Parliament and Government; and not one jot or tittle of the naval security of Britain has been inroaded upon, or whittled upon.

A satisfied Churchill, but a short-sighted one, he would continue to see Ireland as a lapdog, a vassal state – as was evident in his magnanimity of allowing Ireland to have its own navy, provided the natives behaved themselves!

Chapter 10

The Queenstown Outrage

In 1924, as the launch *Wyndham*, carrying British soldiers and dependants from the Cork forts, was being berthed at Cobh, it was the target for a burst of concentrated machine-gun fire. When the rattle of guns had subsided, the havoc wrought by the surprise attack was revealed: one dead and twenty-three injured in various degrees. Quickly, another launch with a doctor, armed soldiers, and a Lewis machine-gun came into the quay to collect all British soldiers on leave. An hour later a second attack on this launch caused a British captain to suffer a flesh wound. During this protracted ambush, further heavy machine-gun fire was sprayed onto the guardship HMS *Scynthe*, anchored at its usual spot in the harbour – happily without casualties.

The attacks occurred on a Friday night when the troops had just been paid and the launch was carrying a larger number of personnel than usual (the ferry boats had a large capacity). The assailants knew this because the ferry timetable was widely publicised. When going on shore leave, British soldiers would be in civilian attire and unarmed – a soft target. The perpetrators of this outrage were from a group of about 150 dissident Republicans who were still hiding out in the mountains about ten miles away from Cobh, even though the Civil War had ended in April of the previous year.

A nationwide manhunt failed to apprehend those responsible. One suspect gave himself up but subsequently withdrew his statement and it was discovered that he was suffering from head wounds inflicted in the earlier hostilities. No further action was taken against him. The Irish Government offered a reward of £10,000 for information leading to the arrest and conviction of any of the assailants: the statement also included the names of five suspects. Eventually seven men were charged but insufficient evidence against them meant that none came to trial.

The casualties included the fourteen-year-old daughter of a Mrs Hayes, the widow of a British naval officer. She got a splinter which blinded her right eye and she suffered thereafter from this; her mother was severely shocked. A bombardier gave evidence that it was impossible for anybody in the launch to see what was happening on the land. The assailants had used the cover of darkness for the attack and to make their escape. One young man received wounds to his body and his right arm had to be amputated: he got compensation of £2,000. Compensation ranged all the way down from that figure to £45 for a slight hand injury. The one fatality was a nineteen-year-old medical orderly from Lancashire who had been killed outright. The badly wounded were evacuated to England for treatment. All British service personnel were now confined to quarters, and the ferry service was restricted to essential duties and guarded by armed soldiers.

News of the outrage was carried in the British and Irish media and indeed internationally. President Cosgrave issued a strong statement saying to the Dáil, 'The motive of the attack was clearly to provoke a diplomatic crisis between the two countries.' Clergy of all denominations condemned the attack: the Bishop of Cork described the ambushers as 'ruffianly cowards', while the Administrator of Cobh's magnificent Protestant cathedral said, 'This was a most un-Christian and un-Irish act, a more cowardly crime never stained the annals of our country before.'

The funeral of the young soldier received massive newspaper coverage and a large Irish Army contingent provided military honours on the day. Virtually the whole population of Cobh attended as the cortège processed through lines of soldiers with arms reversed. Apparently the victim had tossed a coin with a comrade at their headquarters at Chester to see which of them should go on the draft to Cork. He lost the toss, and indeed his life.

The Irish Army placed an armed guard at Cobh and there were no further incidents here. But there were others: earlier, a British War Department launch when passing Blackrock was sprayed with machine-gun fire from the shore and the captain was severely injured. At Fort Templebreedy on the 20 January 1925, a sentry saw two men who opened fire, to which he responded; the alarm was raised, searchlights were switched on and a search party questioned civilians in the vicinity. All these threats contributed to the frayed nerves in the garrisons. Though the local population generally felt no great animosity towards the British presence there was a vehement minority which would freely use force in order to get rid of it. These incidents changed the mindset of the British Army: a report after the Queenstown attack showed a strong reaction to the incident. It underlined the untenable environment of the British presence and in time this may have had some effect on the eventual decision to hand back the forts.

Chapter 11

Inquisitive Visitors

In June 1925, two British officers were despatched to Ireland to check all seven forts in the Free State, and those in Northern Ireland. They were a Lt-Col. Gerard and a Major Grove-White, both war veterans who had won the DSO and were now attached to military intelligence. Grove-White knew Co. Cork very well as his father, another military man, had settled there. Apart from inspecting the coastal forts (there had been no visit since the Treaty had been signed two-and-a-half years earlier) there was a secondary intelligence-gathering element in their mission – their masters wanted an up-to-date assessment of the state of the country. There had been a plan to establish an intelligence network, but this was deemed unnecessary because of regular feedback from the commanders of the forts. This was in the form of secure letters via Royal Navy ships.

The two designated officers crossed on the packet steamer to Cork and began their inspection of the five major forts in the area. They looked at all heavy artillery batteries and their supporting companies of Royal Engineers and the Royal Army Ordnance Corps. The REs maintained the fabric of the forts and the latter attended to repairs of the guns and equipment. Particular regard was given to the number of wireless operators at the various forts – obviously in regard to the transmission of secure radio despatches. They heard a general complaint among the troops that telegrams to their homes, sometimes urgent, were difficult due to the long distance to the nearest civil post office and the high prices charged there. Apparently the army was not prepared to pay for a special line to be laid on to the various forts.

The visitors described Bere Island as a pleasant, scenic location in summer, but out of season it was a wild, lonely and inhospitable place to be stationed. They highlighted the lack of sports facilities, but understood that finance for improving these could not be decided upon until the whole future of the forts was reconsidered. Accommodation was inadequate, though a store had been converted into a dormitory for the officers' servants who were also detailed to act as an armed guard. Provision of married officers' quarters on station was not satisfactory, but there were properties elsewhere that could be rented. The location of the existing married quarters on Bere Island could provide a great temptation for an attack by Republican dissidents and other points were also in danger from snipers. General feeling was that landward defence was at least as important, if not more so, as the main seaward defences.

Regarding Bere Island, the eventual report included, 'If it is to remain part of the coastal defences, the layout of its guns certainly needs to be changed because the current arrangements are archaic and ancient.' It recommended the building of a new battery; an increase of up to three 9.2-inch guns and the relocation and upgrading of some of the 6-inch batteries. However, there was no realistic prospect that these recommendations, costed at over £1 million, would be implemented.

Apart from the British garrisons' necessary contact with certain Irish Army officers, there was no fraternisation between the two forces. The British view was, 'These men have been guilty of ambushes and murders.' Nevertheless, the officer commanding the Southern Ireland Coastal Defences, headquartered at Fort Westmoreland on Spike Island, had exchanged calls with the GOC of the Irish Southern Command, as did

Thirteen years on from the events described in this chapter, Maj. Gen. Brennan, now Chief of Staff, is seen on the right, about to disembark at Spike Island when the coast defense forts were taken back.

Lt-Col. Crerar. Crerar's description of Major General Michael Brennan (a Clare man, later to be Chief-of-Staff) runs as follows:

> He is a man of about 40 who looks younger, the son of a farmer, a resolute and determined man, an active rebel since 1916, and a member of a notorious rebel family. But he took strong measures to maintain law and order in Ireland after the Treaty. He is a very strict disciplinarian, who will stand no nonsense from anyone.

When Brennan returned the British officer's call and visited Spike Island, he was quite keen to learn how proper military messes should be organised and was in favour of young British officers as instructors who would know the state-of-the-art (rather than old retired chaps who wouldn't) to help in

74

setting up the new army. There was nothing condescending in the British officer's assessment of General Brennan, as could have been expected at this time. Colonel Crerar noted that armed Free State troops now awaited the War Department launches which came into Queenstown; this as a result of the fatal incident of the previous year. British and Irish troops were not particularly friendly towards each other but did not go out of their way to cause trouble. There was an earlier British standing order forbidding fraternisation and Crerar felt that this restriction was redundant and should be formally cancelled. He further mentioned that the Free State troops were disciplined and presented a smart appearance. Relations with the public were important as the British troops were stationed in what could be described as oases in what had been enemy territory less than three years earlier. It seemed that friendly relations had been built up with the local authorities and the Garda, the police.

Because of the isolated nature of the forts, garrison personnel complained to the visitors about the lack of female company due to the distance and expense of going into cities and towns. Crerar mentioned that dances in the various forts were well supported by the local lasses, some of whom wished there could be more garrison troops stationed there for these romantic interludes. Looking at this, no doubt through rose-coloured spectacles, the girls gave the impression that the British would be welcomed back. The officers noted that the withdrawal of British forces generally had deeply affected the prosperity of the Cork region. In certain areas relations between soldiers and locals still seemed to be quite fraught as the officers drew a distinction between friendly people and what they described as 'mountainy men'.

Lt-Col. Crerar returned to the UK while Major Grove-White went north to visit the two forts on Lough Swilly. He underlined the isolation of these by noting that a journey into Derry City by a hired car shared out among the troops would cost ten shillings per man each way – a large amount from a squaddie's pay packet. Grove-White felt that official uncertainty about the forts' future and unease regarding yearly reliefs had transmitted itself to the garrison. He also was of the opinion that in the next decade, or even longer, there would be little chance of improving friendliness between the ordinary people of both nations, so deeply entrenched was the anti-British feeling. He mentioned that the Republicans were pretty down-and-out and their funds were low because Americans considered that the Treaty was a fair arrangement and they were now unwilling to send funds as heretofore. Grove-White could not understand why Ireland did not behave in as friendly a way as all the other Dominions. He reflected that, while the Irish Government might be prepared to take over the forts for political kudos, it did not really want them and if they were taken back he felt that their efficiency would suffer. He was very aware that in years to come an attitude of 'England's difficulty is Ireland's opportunity' would still prevail and certainly in the minds of some of the population this was correct as was seen fifteen years later on the outbreak of the Second World War.

Apart from the observations of Major Gore-White, Britain had no military or political intelligence between the wars – there was no diplomatic representation whatsoever in Dublin. Some of the old ascendancy residents sent the most outrageous tales to their contacts across the water, including stories that the IRA was imminently about to take over the country. As a result, Britain had no concept that her erstwhile colony had moved on – this came as a huge shock when the Second World War erupted.

When the visitors' report was received by their GOC in Chester he passed it on to the Undersecretary for War, pointing out that though he agreed with the need for improved landward defences at the forts he did not wish to give the impression that the Irish Government was not in full control of the country.

Chapter 12

Life in the Forts

The British presence in the Irish forts was more than just 'care and maintenance parties', as the gunners were kept on their toes and were capable of springing to action stations at short notice. They were supported by specialists in signalling, mechanics, tradesmen of all kinds, as well as clerks and cooks; a complete backup for a peacetime establishment. Due to the exigencies of military service, the garrisons might not have many men to spare for full-scale practices, but these were expensive in terms of ammunition expenditure and were sometimes curtailed to save money. The garrisons in the five Cork forts totalled about 430 all ranks, including 40 in the Southern Ireland Coastal Defence Headquarters on Spike Island. Adding in the personnel manning the two Lough Swilly forts, that total was just over 800.

Life for the British squaddies was much the same as for their comrades with similar postings in the UK. However there was one great difference – those in Ireland were remote from their own and there were limited opportunities for home leave. No matter where they were based, troops would get twenty-eight days annual leave but for those in Ireland, though not as remote as say India, it took a long time to get home. Thus

Corporal James McLoughlin was a gunner who had seen service on the Western Front during the Great War. Afterwards he was transferred to the Royal Garrison Artillery in Cork Harbour. He described this photograph, 'This is me on a Sunday morning at 8a.m. after being on duty all night.' He subsequently was commissioned in the new Irish National Army where he rose to become a Colonel and the Director of Artillery.

it was more worthwhile to take annual leave as one complete block. Nevertheless, there were breaks from routine. A gunner recollected that, though local leave was sporadic and subject to last minute cancellations, he would take off with a couple of comrades and spend some time in Cork City. He remembered the Bandon Hotel as a small, clean, and well-run place where one could get a bed and a generous well-cooked breakfast for the equivalent of 17½p per night, which was all a private soldier could afford. The Bandon was noted for its good supply of hot water, which was not always available on Spike Island – except when the top brass were carrying out periodic inspections!

A young, newly-qualified wireless operator in the Royal Signal Corps was quite excited when, in 1934, he was posted to Ireland. Early in

August he arrived at Spike Island which, for the next two years, would be his military home. He reported:

The Signal Section proved to be even smaller than I had expected. We were attached to the Royal Artillery in an RA Coastal Defence Brigade that made up the bulk of the garrison, together with a few other units such as a company of the Royal Engineers stationed at Fort Camden. Spike boasted a small military hospital with the usual medical staff, together with other support units from other corps. But life revolved around the gunners – it was their show. The main function of our Section was to provide wireless communications between the various forts, with our base at Catterick Camp, and with the Royal Navy's destroyer anchored in the harbour. It was known as 'the guardship' and would now and then up-anchor to patrol the surrounding coastal waters and make a visit to Berehaven.

Official despatches were not our only transmissions: we were constantly chatting but this was not regarded as a security risk even though we used English rather than code. One had only to tune into the BBC to hear us, indeed listeners to its programmes constantly complained about us blotting them out and ruining their enjoyment! The Navy's standard of wireless operating was very high and their equipment was much more up-to-date than ours. In the fort, our distance from the moored destroyer was only about a mile and its very powerful transmitter nearly blew our heads off. The aerial masts on Spike were erected on the ramparts: the system was vast and to the layman it must have appeared as a web of tangled wires. When the gunners were carrying out their practice shoots against targets out at sea, our duty was to co-operate with their own signals section in providing wireless communications between the target-towing boat and the guns.

There was now a submarine cable connecting the telephone exchange at Spike with the civilian post office at Cobh so phone calls were possible as the UK Security was non-existent and there were no 'scrambling' devices. As specialists we escaped such routine chores as spud-bashing, fire guard, and sentry duties. Spike had limited sporting facilities: we had two indoor tennis courts and though part of the parade ground was marked out for hockey there was no football or rugby ground. Our swimming pool was provided by the sea. As a keen swimmer, and quite a strong one, I swam in the surrounding waters where the tides were swift and the currents often dangerous. Against all standing orders, on a swimming outing I once swam away from our boat heading for the mainland when I got into serious difficulties. The sergeant in charge of the boat saw me and saved me just in time. On being revived I was given a right rollicking for being so foolish. Apart from being very scared I could have jeopardised the fun and pleasure of the others if the boat had been withdrawn. Indeed, if the sergeant had not agreed to hush up the incident I could have come before a Court of Inquiry.

For going ashore there was a reliable ferry service. The boat steamed in a straight line from the jetty at Spike to the pier at Cobh in about twenty minutes; though at low tide it had to make a detour which added about another twenty minutes to the journey. The ferry boats were about the size of a small coastal tug and could take quite a large number of passengers. They flew the blue ensign of the War Office and the crews were mostly Irish civilians. Even if on duty, we were forbidden to travel to the mainland in uniform but everybody there knew we were British soldiers because of our haircuts and highly-polished shoes. We mingled easily with civilians in their pubs and at dances and we played them at sport – some of the lads even married Irish girls. If there was any division between Catholics and Protestants I never noticed it, for life was peaceful and there were no experiences of disquiet or apprehension.

In the forts there were dances which could take place in the Officers' Mess, the Warrant Officers' and Sergeants' Mess, or the All Ranks' Mess. They were all rather formal; soldiers would wear their best blues uniform and the ladies would usually be in evening dress. The dances were quite glittering affairs though the numbers were not very large because it was difficult to find enough girls. The officers' wives always attended, and girl-friends from Cobh and Cork would receive personal invitations. It was not all dancing; many a girl was invited to take a stroll on the ramp, to see the view. At the less glamorous end of the scale, life was neither soft nor easy and indeed in some respects it was poor. Our barrack room was dark, dingy and damp, and the standard of food was appalling. But as signalmen we had better conditions than the others, though we worked long hours and endured the usual kit inspections, arms inspections, medical inspections, barrack room inspections, and so on, and so on.

In the early autumn of each year, postings began to come in for those who were earmarked for overseas during the coming trooping season. One day my number came up as follows, 'Posted to 1st Indian Division Signals, Rawalpindi, India' – and my time in the soft Irish air was over.

Chapter 13

A New Agreement

De Valera formed Fianna Fáil in 1926, a new party which became a brisk political machine. This ensured that it was able to form a coalition government in 1932, before winning outright control in the following year. Britain was dismayed that the losers in the Civil War should emerge triumphant at the polls and this followed a deep suspicion of Dev and his Republicans. This was with good reason too, as Dev immediately began a campaign to dismantle the country's dominion status, removing the office of the Governor General and any other trappings which gave the appearance of Ireland as anything less than a sovereign independent state. A new constitution in 1937 consolidated this status.

In Britain in the mid-1930s, Malcolm McDonald, the Dominions Secretary and Neville Chamberlain, the Prime Minister, were both very anxious to settle all the outstanding matters of friction, including trade disputes, between the two countries. At this time the thinking on the defence of the UK was changing, some in its armed forces were now willing to talk about withdrawing from the Treaty ports and forts in the expectation of improved relations – but not the Royal Navy.

At the beginning of 1938 the British chiefs-of-staff had been asked to advise on the following questions. For what purpose was it intended to employ the defended ports in Ireland in the event of a major war? The top brass responded:

> It would be most desirable to use Queenstown [Cobh], Lough Swilly, Berehaven and Kingstown [Dún Laoghaire] as bases for both mine-sweeping and anti-submarine hunting. Berehaven would be vital should Portsmouth prove untenable. The temporary transfer of the Grand Fleet from Scapa Flow to Lough Swilly in 1914 showed the desirability of maintaining alternative bases. In preparing plans for trade protection, the Admiralty has always counted upon the use of the ports in Ireland. It had to have control of the ports for two good reasons. First, to use them themselves; secondly, to deny them to the enemy.

The next question was, if the ports remain in UK hands, and if, on the outbreak of war, Ireland was to adopt a hostile attitude, would the ports be of sufficient importance to warrant the additional measures necessary to ensure their security? To which they replied:

> To prevent the ports, as they stood, being captured by Ireland, one infantry brigade per port, plus a division with AA defences for the hinterland would be required. To regain the ports would be a more formidable operation than the reinforcement of existing garrisons. It would be comparable to the Gallipoli landing– at least three divisions would be required, and it could be an impossible mission.

> [Gallipoli was one of Winston Churchill's misadventures in the Great War: author.]

The last major question was, 'If the ports had been handed over to Ireland and if, on the outbreak of war, Ireland were to deny their use, would the importance of the ports be so great as to warrant military operations to regain them?' The answer was that when it came to securing the ports the use of force should not be excluded, even if it meant the complete reoccupation of Ireland to prevent its territory being used as a base for hostile action, either by submarines or aircraft, against Britain or Northern Ireland.

Chamberlain sent a note to McDonald saying:

I am not sure that I appreciate the use which the General Staff think we should want to make of the Irish ports in war'. Later he said, 'I fully understand the danger if they were used by enemy forces, but of course there would be a wide difference between an assurance that no enemy could use them, and an assurance that we should have the use of them for any purpose we liked. I think any reference to the chiefs-of-staff should bring out this point. We would get the first assurance, but not the second, and I should like to feel satisfied as to the importance of the difference.

To this the military men responded, 'No effort should be spared to ensure that friendly relations with Ireland are maintained, even if that involves extending the rights over the reserved ports.' This of course meant returning them.

Very shortly thereafter, negotiations with the Irish Government began. There were matters, other than the ports and forts, to be discussed. The Economic War (which Britain preferred to call a 'financial dispute') had greatly penalised Irish exports, and had to be settled. Additionally, future trade arrangements between the two countries had to be negotiated. On the question of the ports, the British side was divided, but Chamberlain and McDonald carried the day. McDonald found De Valera to be tough and stern throughout the discussions; however, on a personal level, they were cordial and respected each other. De Valera repeatedly emphasised that the ports would not necessarily be available to the Royal Navy in wartime. Also, as he had previously done in both 1935 and 1936, he again guaranteed that Ireland would never allow itself to be used as a base from which to attack Britain. A new Agreement was signed which unambiguously rendered the 1921 Treaty redundant. There were no conditions whatsoever regarding the use of the ports by anyone, in peace or in war, save the Irish State.

In Ireland, the result of the negotiations was generally seen as a triumph – but not within the ranks of Unionists and militant Republicans, for very different reasons! The Agreement was generally popular with the British press and in political circles also, one exception being Winston Churchill. He was then in the political wilderness, but gave his reaction during the House of Commons debate on the issue. His anger was directed at the prospective wartime diminution of British naval operating range represented by the denial of the ports. Churchill had been one of the principal architects of the Anglo-Irish Treaty which de Valera had successfully eroded. He declared:

These ports are in fact 'the sentinel towers' of the western approaches, by which the 45 million in this island so enormously depend on foreign food for their daily bread, and by which they carry on their trade, which is equally important to their existence. We are to give them up, unconditionally, to an Irish Government led by men – I do not want to use hard words – whose rise to power has been proportionate to the animosity with which they have acted against this country, no doubt in pursuance of their own patriotic impulses and whose position in power is based upon the violation of solemn Treaty engagements.

ÉIRE

TREATY SERIES, 1938
No. 1

AGREEMENTS

BETWEEN THE

Government of Ireland

AND THE

Government of the United Kingdom

London, April 25, 1938.

Approved by Dáil Eireann, April 29, 1938.

PRESENTED TO BOTH HOUSES OF THE OIREACHTAS BY
THE MINISTER FOR EXTERNAL AFFAIRS.

DUBLIN
PUBLISHED BY THE STATIONERY OFFICE.

To be purchased directly from the
GOVERNMENT PUBLICATIONS SALE OFFICE, 3—4, COLLEGE STREET,
DUBLIN, or through any Bookseller.

Price Sixpence.

(P. No. 3104.)

He could not take in that a new mutual agreement had been signed. Churchill then asked, what guarantee did Britain have that 'Southern Ireland' would not declare neutrality if Britain was engaged in war with a powerful nation? Chamberlain did not give any answer to this but it was an odds-on certainty that Éire would declare its neutrality for many good and valid reasons.

But de Valera, who had ceaselessly, but unavailingly, argued the case for ending partition during the negotiations, saw the shadow of things to come in his last letter to Chamberlain:

> I cannot refrain from writing to you. You and I have worked to bring about conditions which would make it possible to lay the foundations of good neighbourly relations between the British and the Irish peoples. The agreement, a year ago, was a notable advance in that direction; but the failure to deal with Partition has largely offset what was then accomplished. A free united Ireland would have every interest in wishing Britain to be strong, but when Britain's strength appears to be used to maintain the division of our island no such consideration can have any force: a large section of our people, particularly the young, are led to see hope only in Britain's weakness. Can something not be done, and without delay?

The wartime attitude of the Irish people might have altered if it had been possible to 'do something' and the thirty years of carnage post war would have been avoided.

Chapter 14

Preparations

With the Agreement signed, a series of detailed conferences on its implementation began at the office of the Irish High Commissioner in London. The minutiae of what would, and what would not, be transferred, had to be agreed. The Irish delegation was not happy about such items as the 12-pounder guns, which it felt were part of the fixed defences and should be free of charge. The British were somewhat hazy about this; there were eight usable weapons and the interpretation of Article 2 of the Agreement had to be settled. There was a number of 4.5-inch howitzers at Berehaven and Lough Swilly, these being mobile, rather than fixtures, were purchased and used to equip field batteries.

The War Office put forward other matters including the best method of effecting the transfer of the various forts and the dates when this should take place. The British mentioned 31 December 1938 but the Irish side preferred 11 July (the seventeenth anniversary of the 1921 truce, now an army holiday) for the transfer of the Cork Harbour sites, and this was agreed. It was further noted, 'There are certain squash courts, garages, etc. which have been provided out of private or regimental funds. What are the views in regard to taking these over?' – they were purchased. The British side also raised the question of what prospects could be offered to the local crews who manned the launches of the War Department fleet and to other civilian employees, but this matter was left open. A significant query was raised regarding whether the army would take over the existing defence plans of the forts, or would they make out their own schemes? A very firm yes was the answer, because of the British experience.

During the discussions, it was noted that one of the 9.2-inch guns at Templebreedy had a cracked tube and that another was suffering from steel choke. These faults could not be remedied before 11 July but it would be done afterwards, the cost being borne by the Britain. A training course was arranged and two British officers and twenty-four other ranks, all volunteers, would be offered inducements to remain in post for six months.

At the conclusion, the British representatives expressed thanks for the speedy action that the Irish side was taking in all matters – everything was settled. The important question of manning the forts, a completely new undertaking for the army, had been planned as far back as January 1937, when a recruiting drive had been started.

At the beginning of 1938 the Committee of Imperial Defence had estimated that it would cost approximately £650,000 to modernise the Treaty forts: anti-submarine booms, indicator loops, and proper anti-aircraft defences were required. At Lough Swilly, the pair of 9.2-inch guns at Lenane Fort required modernisation, and a new signal station on Dunaff Head was required to replace one that had been burnt down. These improvements were not undertaken and the forts stayed in a rather sub-standard condition throughout the war, though the army undertook limited improvements.

Following on from the London talks, army officers began to take inventory of what the newly formed Coast Defence branch of the

1938: A new barrel is being hauled along the Western Avenue in Cork City *en route* to Fort Templebreedy to replace a faulty one on a 9.2-inch gun. This was a sizeable task for both the steam engine and the gunners.

Artillery Corps would shortly take over. Since 1922 the forts' garrisons had been much more than just 'care-and-maintenance parties' – a few craftsmen keeping the guns well greased and oiling machinery generally. Peacetime garrisons had been maintained and the installations were operational.

However, as mentioned, these did not represent the state-of-the-art, which would have required improved mountings for the guns, anti-aircraft weapons, and protection from belligerent aircraft. Also, the naval facilities which the forts guarded required considerable

A British instructor fraternises with
one of his Irish pupils, 1938.

expenditure before they too could be brought up to scratch, but with
a small embryonic Marine Service planned, Ireland only required
the existing facilities on Haulbowline Island close to Spike Island.

Chapter 15

Who will man the guns?

On a bright July day in 1938 Cork City was *en fête*. Four army bands playing well-known marches such as 'O'Donnell Abú', 'Clare's Dragoons' and 'The Dawning of the Day', accentuated the stamp of a thousand marching men. This was the culmination of the negotiations of 1937/38 which resulted in the handing back of the Treaty forts. This agreement, of course, raised the question, who would man the mighty guns and complex equipment in the forts? The marching men represented the answer.

In the 1930s the Army had shrunk to its lowest strength ever, but it did incorporate a small Artillery Corps whose members considered themselves to be the cream of the force. These men were proficient with field guns, howitzers, and anti-aircraft weapons, but none, as yet, was experienced in the heavier static weapons in the coastal forts. In October 1937 a limited recruiting drive began and continued until April 1938. For young Irishmen at the time, economic recession caused large-scale unemployment or emigration. Joining the Army was an alternative.

An old gunner speaks of the choice he made:

I was eighteen in January 1938 and went to the local Garda barracks to enlist. Having passed the education and medical tests, I was taken by lorry, together with some other recruits picked up at various stations, and we eventually arrived at the main army base at the Curragh in Co. Kildare. There we were 'processed': kitted out in uniforms and equipment and given our army numbers – mine was 76567 which is what is called a palindrome as it reads the same both ways. My fellow recruits represented all parts of Ireland and we were formed into a platoon of forty.

What an awkward lot we were when we started learning drill on the large square. When we fell out for a break we could see that earlier recruits had already learned great precision in marching and arms drill. All the NCO instructors were grand men, there was no bullying, they led us but never drove us. All recruits were just over 18 years of age and we were told that after 4 weeks basic training we would go to whichever branch of the army we preferred. But first, we had to complete our basic course which included firing our brand new Lee Enfield rifles. We had sports every day: football, hurling, running, jumping … but there was no escaping the constant 'square bashing'. At last, looking like real soldiers, we finished basic training just as recruiting ended and the last recruits started their training.

Then our lot were sized off. A chalk line at 5ft 8ins was drawn on a wall and anyone who could reach it or was even taller could go to the Artillery Corps. From the recruiting intake there were over 1,000 of us and 360, myself included, were tall enough to be coastal gunners. We handed in our webbing equipment which was replaced with leather bandoliers and white lanyards, and the fine brass collar badges which marked us out as gunners.

We tackled our new gear in order to become what was known in the army as 'jildy files', the ultimate in military smartness. The uniform was dark green with a high collar tunic, peaked cap, riding breeches and leg-

93

In pre-War days, the Artillery Corps gunners, seen here in the Phoenix Park, wore the smartest of uniforms.

gings and the old-timers were willing to teach us lads how to get the best out of it. Boots were important: first, the brown dye was scraped off until white leather appeared; then a good scrub with soap and boiling water got rid of all traces of oil and preservatives; next, a rub with fine sandpaper would give a short fuzzy nap. No less than ten coats of red ink, applied over a week, gave the necessary base onto which ruby-red polish was beaten and boned in, with the back of an old toothbrush while all was kept moist with spit. The result: a mirror-like finish and a thing of beauty. The jildy artilleryman gave the same care to his bandolier and would bring up his white lanyard with Blanco. Steel spurs had their pointed ends cut with a hacksaw and silver three-penny pieces would be fitted into the grooves, which added a jaunty jingle.

We paraded in our best uniforms when we were minutely scrutinised for fit and the brilliance of our leather accoutrements. We had earlier learnt that there was a certain type of leather bandolier which took a marvellous shine and this was the kind we had picked out from the array in the quartermaster's stores. Now our NCOs gave us three days of lectures on different types of guns and we learnt how to move these about as a team and were told why some had long barrels and others had short ones. On the fourth

Irish gunners fire one of the 9.2-inch guns at Fort Templebreedy, 1940.

day we were told, 'You are the young men who, from the start, were picked out for a particular assignment, manning the coastal defence forts. We are not sending out experienced field artillery gunners because they would have to unlearn all that they had learnt over the years. You will find that there is a great difference between the gun drill and tactics that you have learnt so far and for the big weapons you will now serve'.

On the 4 July 1938 we all marched the three miles to Kildare station and onto a special train. Off we went non-stop to Glanmire station where we fell in behind the bands, and had a memorable march to Collin's Barracks in the City. All the wide streets were free of traffic and were covered with bunting and flags; the great crowds of onlookers spilled off the pavements and left us just enough room to march through. The cheering was so loud we could hardly hear the bands' music; all we could hear was the beat of the

Manhandling a gun at the Curragh Camp in 1940, with one of the crew straddling the barrel, as a counterweight. Some would go on to serve on bigger weapons at the coastal forts.

big drums. On we marched, and all the teenage girls were screaming, point-ing and shouting: 'Look at the pawnees.' The lads wondered: 'What is a pawnee, isn't it an Indian tribe?' Our Cork comrades enlightened us: appar-ently the word in Cork means an enamel mug. These were hanging from our haversacks and bumping off our buttocks, so we obviously marched with a very sexy wiggle. When our sergeants couldn't see we overdid the wiggle and all the girls went crazy, all the way up the hill to the barracks.

PORT of CORK

The Latin slogan of the Arms of Cork Harbour proclaims, 'A Safe Harbour for Ships'. The aerial view shows a vessel which has just entered this splendid anchorage. (*Images courtesy of the Port of Cork Company.*)

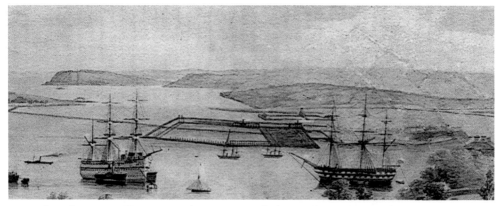

Over the course of his career, Robert Lowe Stopford painted several views of Cork Harbour. The largest of these dates from the late 1870s and measures 6ft. This detail shows the eastern side of the harbour as viewed from Cobh. The complete painting adorns the headquarters of the Port of Cork Company and this detail is reproduced by courtesy of that body.

Cork Harbour, *c.*1862. This detail of a painting by George M.W. Atkinson which shows a two-decker ship of the line flying a white ensign, with a French schooner in the left background. In the right background, another ship of the line is flying signal flags. (*Courtesy of Crawford Municipal Gallery.*)

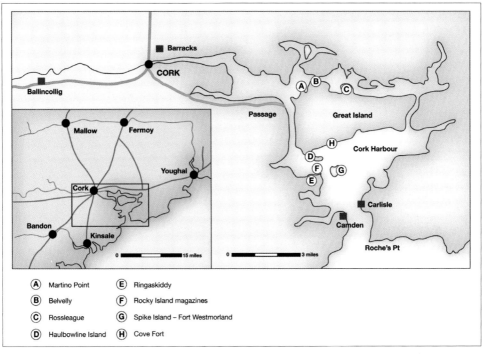

The complex geography of Cork's great harbour and its relation to the surrounding county is shown here. On the extreme left of the larger map, Ballincollig Powder Mills provided a convenient stock of explosives for the earlier cannon based at Spike Island (G), and at Camden and Carlisle.

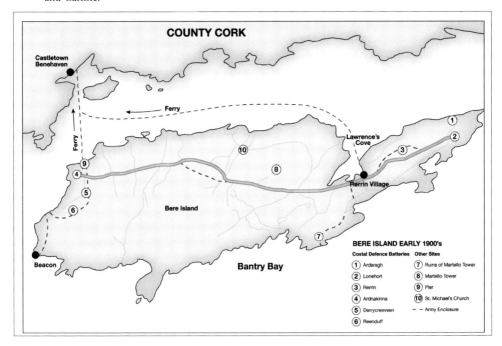

The sheltered waters between the mainland and Bere Island were of great strategic value and this was recognised by the various gun emplacements that protected this anchorage.

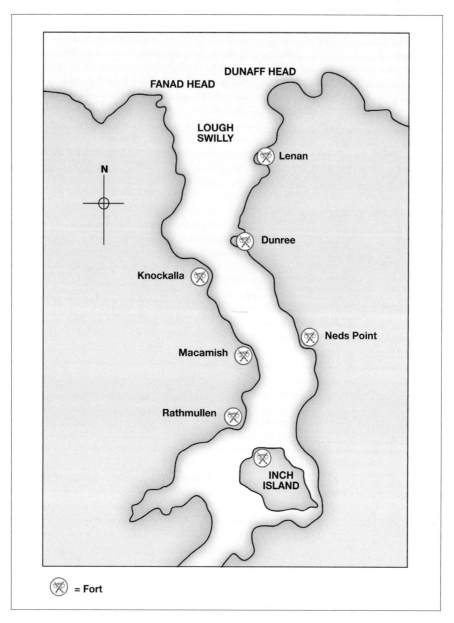

DUNAFF HEAD

FANAD HEAD

LOUGH SWILLY

(⊗) Lenan

N

(⊗) Dunree

Knockalla (⊗)

(⊗) Neds Point

Macamish (⊗)

Rathmullen (⊗)

(⊗)
INCH ISLAND

(⊗) = Fort

In the north of the country, the deep anchorage of Lough Swilly penetrated for twenty-five miles, virtually up to Letterkenny. Over the centuries the coastal forts saw many changes and today, luckily, the major fort at Dunree, with its splendid museum, is an example of how coast artillery developed down the centuries. This map shows the situation in 1902, when Fort Lenan had just been completed. Before this, in 1891, the three forts on the west side were declared redundant, though their sites remained unarmed and unoccupied. Artillery had improved to the extent that the guns of the four forts on the opposite shore could now cover the entire lough.

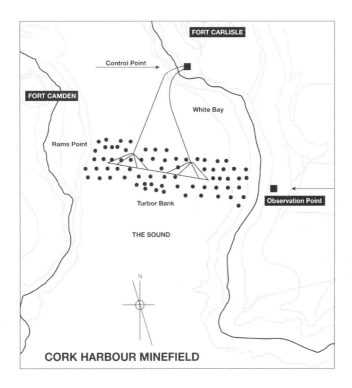

Near the mouth of Cork Harbour in 1941, the Infant Marine Service laid a series of huge electrically controlled mines, which were sown at varying depths. This data was shown in the control point and the most suitable mine or mines could be exploded from information delivered to the controllers from the observation point.

This painting by contemporary artist Kenneth King depicts MTBs of the Irish Marine Service during the Second World War emerging from Dalkey Sound during an exercise. (*Courtesy Mr & Mrs S. Wall.*)

The basic layout of Fort Carlisle (Fort Davis) remained virtually unchanged since its construction in the mid-nineteenth century. Nature's rugged coastline protected the fort on one side, while on the landward perimeter a deep man-made ditch would deter enemies.

This aerial view shows Fort Westmoreland, renamed Fort Mitchel, sited on Spike Island. It is the only 'star' or 'bastion' fort that has been continually occupied throughout the centuries. Plans are currently being made to convert the fort into a museum, detailing its long history.

The only surviving example of the mighty 9.2-inch coast defence gun is seen here at the Imperial War Museum's display at Duxford Aerodrome, Cambridgeshire.

This 4.7-inch gun, which was originally positioned on Bere Island, is now on view at Fort Dunree Museum, suitably preserved against the elements. In its operational life it would have been camouflaged in grey and green, as would all the other coast guns.

Above: A rehearsal for a salute. On the actual day the gunners would don their No.1 uniforms.

Left: Former members of Fort Meagher's garrison stand stiffly at attention as the Tricolour is lowered for the last time, in May 1986.

Below: Despite the grand plans outlined by the authorities at the 1986 ceremony, Fort Meagher remains totally neglected today and is steadily decaying.

Chapter 16

The Changing of the Guard

Another survivor of the original coastal gunners picks up the story where his comrade left off:

When the parade was drawn up on the square in Collins Barracks we were addressed by the Director of our Corps, he said, 'You young men are making history, this is the first time we ever got anything from Britain without shedding blood for it. You are all too young to remember those times for you were only babies then.'

'The people of Cork's own rebel town want to give you the freedom of the City. They will recognise you by your collar badges and bandoliers as gunners. There are places out there in the City which are out-of-bounds to troops, but you won't know them and the Redcaps (the military police) will not interfere with you if you behave yourselves and don't let the side down. The rest of this day is your own and your only duty tomorrow will be church parade at 0900 hours.'

The Major was right and the freedom of the city meant that everything was on the house for the weekend, as three of us soon discovered. Out on the street we met some of our pals who told us that a bus conductor would not take their fares. Off went the three of us to the cinema which was showing *Follies of 1938* and they let us in for free. Afterwards, we had huge wafers from the 'Stop Me and Buy One' ice cream man who wouldn't take payment either. Next we went into a pub, though we didn't drink then, and here too the soft drinks were on the house. We tried to buy some sweets but the man behind the counter forestalled us, 'Here lads, have some bars of chocolate on me.'

Monday, the great day, dawned and the various detachments formed up. Some travelled by train and others by lorry, as we, who were destined for Fort Carlisle, did. As we passed through towns and villages the people were out cheering us and we all waved back in the spirit of the day. On arrival I noticed that the sentries from our advance parties had taken post. There were still British troops in the fort and during dinner we were told that we must stay in our barracks rooms until it was time for the ceremonies. By then it was a lovely warm July evening with some light clouds occasionally shading the sun. At 1740 hours we fell in and marched to our position facing the British troops on one side of the flagpole where the Union Jack was fluttering. We could see that the Brits were all older than us but they were all tall men, just like us – you had to be tall for coastal artillery action drill.

When the British flag was lowered on Spike Island at 20.00 hours precisely, An Taoiseach slowly raised the Tricolour.

This was the signal to all the other forts to raise our flag and on Carlisle, as it climbed slowly we presented arms, as did the British troops, all to the sound of bugles. Strangely, a sudden burst of sunlight caught the flag – perhaps an omen? The whole atmosphere was dramatic: car horns were blowing everywhere and the sound of sirens was heard from all the ships in the harbour. After the ceremonies, we all went out to the local village of Whitegate where the locals welcomed us profusely and said how they appreciated what had been achieved that day – surely a great day.

A historic moment: the changing of the guard at Spike Island, 11 July 1938, as British gunners hand over their headquarters to the Irish Army.

Fort Westmoreland, Spike Island, 11 July 1938. Outside the guard house the British guard stands down as Irish gunners take post.

Green in: before the handover, the Irish garrison marches in.

Khaki out: Fort Mitchel, Spike Island, 11 July 1938. The British garrison leaves to embark for the UK. The last man is carrying the Union Jack.

Taoiseach Eamon De Valera inspects a guard of honour on Spike Island at the handing over of the Treaty Ports.

Final farewell: HMS *Acosta*, which served as the guardian in Cork Harbour for many years, leaves Cork Harbour for the last time as the Treaty Forts are handed back in July 1938. Two years later this warship was sunk in Churchill's ill-concieved 'adventure' in Norway. Only one member of its crew survived.

Chapter 17

Other Ceremonies

Formal events on the evening before the take-over ceremonies were described by Lt-Col. R. Love who commanded the British headquarters on Spike Island. His account was published in *The Journal of the Royal Artillery*:

'Mr Vice, the President of Éire.' For the first time in history this toast was given out by the mess president in a Royal Artillery Mess, immediately after 'The King' had been drunk. The occasion was the last regimental guest night to be held in the RA Mess, Spike Island. The guests of honour were Col. McCabe and five other officers of the Éireann Defence Forces from Collins Barracks, Cork, all in full dress.

The scene now changes to Cork City Barracks. Fifteen British officers in mess kit, having being driven there in Irish Army cars from Queenstown, were dining in the old mess room as the guests of Mr Frank Aiken, the Minister of Defence. Maj.-Gen. Brennan and all the more senior officers of the Éireann Southern Command were present. At the conclusion of dinner, Mr Aiken rose and first in Irish and then in English proposed 'His Majesty

The Royal Artillery garrison from Fort Westmoreland marches down the quay to embark for Britain.

King George', while the band played the full sixteen bars of our national anthem. This was followed by the OC, Southern Irish Coast Defences, proposing 'The President of Éire', which in turn was drunk with musical honours.

These two incidents illustrate possibly better than anything else the very great change that has taken place in the relationships between the two forces. Ever since the first conference in May at the office of the High Commissioner in London, Mr Dulanty, which was followed by a 3-day conference on Spike Island a fortnight later, it was obvious that the Irish representatives were all out to help and to make the task of the transfer of the defences and the evacuation of the troops as easy as it humanly could be. This willingness to co-operate was fully reciprocated by the British with the result that the necessary work was greatly facilitated. These two conferences not only settled matters of principle but to a large extent helped in matters of detail. Works which have been in occupation for over 100 years have accumulated masses of stores of all kinds, quite apart from the actual defences to be handed over as per the Agreement and these cannot be moved at a moment's notice. When it is remembered that the mainland was not available for transport, that everything had to be moved by water and that at each fort there was only one small hand crane at the end of each pier and that sea and tide frequently rendered coming alongside difficult if not impossible, then some idea will be obtained of the amount of detail that had to be considered.

Various lists were formed: stores to be handed over free, stores to be evacuated, stores to be sold or handed over at a valuation, engineers' stores, barrack stores, signal stores, garrison, regimental and unit stores, mess property, church property, NAAFI [the British forces' civilian supermarket]. One curious fact was discovered, that of the pews in the Garrison church at Spike: part were on charge to barracks while the rest were Engineer stores, but all were exactly alike, equally narrow and equally hard. Also it is a question which were kept busiest during those six weeks: the typewriters or the vessels of the War Dept fleet!

Thanks to the Irish representatives agreeing to take over a considerable amount, things were not as difficult as they might have been, though owing to the date of the transfer being advanced from 31 December to 11 July there was not much time to spare. Problems were solved or solved themselves, stores were evacuated, married families sent off and the garrison gradually reduced to the numbers that could be accommodated on board the MV *Innisfallen*.

With the help of fatigue parties provided by both British and Irish personnel and overtime working by the already overworked WD fleet, all problems were overcome. For the personnel of the latter no praise is too high for the way in which, in the circumstances in which they were placed, both British and Irish ratings carried out the additional work on which depended the smooth working of all the arrangements for the handing over. After the ceremonies on Spike Island the British troops marched

Fort Dunree, 26 October 1938. Newly arrived Irish gunners fraternise with their opposite numbers from the Royal Artillery who are about to depart, together with their mascot.

straight down to the pier, headed by the Éireann Army band playing 'The British Grenadiers' and embarked on the tender lying alongside the pier, a considerable number of Irish officers and men following them down to see the troops off.

At 1845 hrs the MV *Innisfallen* was sighted coming down the river, the tender left the pier and as the last hawser was cast off, the Eireann band on the pier, which had been playing selections, played our National Anthem right through. All officers stood at the salute, all NCOs and men at attention and every civilian within sight or hearing, either on the pier or in boats or vessels nearby, had his hat off. There was no need for anyone to call for cheers from the British troops in reply to this compliment. As the tender passed the drill shed on Spike Island a salute of 21 guns was fired from a battery of four 18 pdr guns manned by Éireann troops. When the tender came alongside the *Innisfallen*, the latter paid the compliment of dipping her ensign. If, as an Irish officer had a few days before remarked to the writer, what they wanted was to 'give the departing British troops a really good send-off, where not one man would leave with even the suspicion of a nasty taste in the mouth', they certainly succeeded.

After these ceremonies in Cork the remaining Treaty forts were taken over: Bere Island in September and the Lough Swilly forts in the following month. In mid-September the British Prime Minister Neville Chamberlain, had flown to Munich to appease Hitler who was now sabre-rattling about the Sudeten areas of Czechoslovakia. Chamberlain returned, waving a piece of paper which he said guaranteed, 'Peace in our time'. The diplomatic tension which now gripped Europe translated itself into a curious hitch on Bere Island which was, as somebody said, 'about as far away from Munich that one could get and still be in Europe'.

On 26 September an advance party of Irish gunners arrived at the island to be followed shortly by a group of sixty. The British troops were still loading their gear when their commander received a signal to stop the proceedings. On hearing this, the government in Dublin sent a peremptory message that the Union Jack was to be hauled down by nightfall. After a two-hour delay the British recommenced their embarkation preparations. Now there was a hand-over ceremony at Rerren Redoubt, the main defence installation – but no government representatives attended and no local dignatories had been invited. There was no official photographer – however a local clergyman recorded the event on his 'Box Brownie' camera.

There was due ceremony: full strength guards-of-honour provided by both sides and martial music and anthems were played by an army band in full dress. Its conductor looked so splendid that a British officer took him to be of exalted rank and showed him due deference, until he took up his baton.

The Union Jack was lowered and the Tricolour hoisted, the British flag being presented to the Irish commander as a memento. He duly

Fort Berehaven, 20 September 1938. The outgoing British troops, together with the Irish newcomers, render honours as the Tricolour is hoisted.

signed himself into the Officers' Mess record book, writing his name and that of his unit in Irish. Later, when the officer was checking the files, he found some interesting documents which had been left behind. Dated 1920, they were in a British Army intelligence file which listed the names of local families who were actively pro-British. It also included a list of IRA men who were to be arrested and have their property burned in reprisal raids. The loss of these incriminating papers was discovered and somewhat shamefaced, the owners requested their return, but they had already been sent on to army archives and could not be made available. When questioned in later years about the sudden glitch in the handover, the erstwhile Dominions Secretary, Malcolm McDonald, was rather vague, but he did say that perhaps the missing documents had been the cause of the hitch in the takeover arrangements. Who knows?

On a wet and windy day in October 1938 there was a brief ceremony as the 5th Coastal Battery of the Irish Army took over from the outgoing British garrison. A half-dozen members from each side rendered honours as a bugler sounded General Salute.

When the Lough Swilly forts were taken over on a rainy day in October, the music was limited to bugle calls and the guards-of-honour consisted of half-a-dozen men from each side. The British sergeant who lowered the Union Jack and the Irish sergeant who raised the Tricolour at Dunree were brothers-in-law. Though modest, it was a most amiable ceremony and when completed, the British gunners boarded lorries and were driven across the Border to the railway station in Derry. Two of the newly formed coastal defence units now took charge: the 5th Battery at Dunree and the 6th Battery at Fort Lenan.

Chapter 18

Neutrality

In 1932, the Government of Ireland had passed from one alignment of the Civil War to the opposing side, in a spirit of peaceful democracy. The people of Ireland had little time for either the Nazi regime developing in Germany or the Communists. After years of strife, they wanted no part in the wars of the great powers – a position repeatedly expressed by their government. The general feeling about the Nazis was exemplified in 1938 when the Lord Mayor of Cork refused to welcome a visit by a German warship to his city. In the country at large, perhaps the presence of its neighbour's powerful navy engendered a sense of security from such remote foreign threats, reinforced by the eventual settlement with Britain, which included the return of the coastal forts. Now there was only one outstanding irritation, partition. There was a downside to this false sense of security: despite warnings from the Army General Staff in 1936, the Defence Forces were still woefully neglected, and after the collapse of France in 1940 the country was wide open to invasion by either side.

At the beginning of the war there were strongly held opinions regarding neutrality. The Crown Forces, including the Black and Tans, had

The German battle-cruiser *Schleswig-Holstein* visited Cork Harbour in 1938. No doubt cameras were clicking as the vessel passed the Cork forts. However, the Lord Mayor of the city was aware of the Nazi regime of the time and refused to welcome the crew.

only departed some sixteen years earlier and memories were still quite vivid. The basic and overriding reason for Irish neutrality, completely misunderstood in Britain, was that the country had subsumed the idea of neutrality into sovereignty which for so many centuries had been denied. It cannot be said too strongly, the vast majority of Irish people wanted nothing to do with the war of the great powers. The country was now a free, independent, sovereign state and impervious to the influence of any larger country.

There were many reasons for this stance. The losses suffered by the country in the Great War were still remembered and in the words of one historian had an effect 'akin to the Great Famine'. More than 200,000 Irishmen had fought in that war, all of them volunteers. At the Islandbridge Memorial Gardens in Dublin's Phoenix Park the figure for those who fell is given as 49,435. When the new war broke out, Britain fully expected the Irish Government, despite the 1938 Agreement, to meekly hand back the ports and the forts and, indeed, many other facilities which had never been mentioned previously. In the early hours of 3 September, before Chamberlain made his dreaded announcement, the Dáil rushed through an Emergency Powers Bill to secure the preservation of the State. Neutrality was an all-party commitment as government and opposition knew only too well that if the country supported Britain, one result could well be internal strife with the IRA. This illegal organisation was currently planting bombs in Britain, and even though the government clamped down heavily on the IRA, it remained a threat throughout the war. Older people in particular, with memories of the Civil War, had a deep fear that Irish engagement on the side of Britain could easily lead to a recurrence of that bitter struggle from whose shadow Ireland was still trying to emerge.

Another practical reason: the army numbered fewer than 20,000 all ranks: to be specific, it was 19,136 strong, made up of 7,600 Regulars, 4,300 AB Reservists, and 7,236 men of the Volunteer Force which had been established in 1934 as a part-time territorial reserve. All were soon involved in brisk collective training until the parsimonious Department of Finance advised the government that it could not justify any greater strength than the peacetime figures – even though at this level, the forces were only at 50 per cent of establishment. Since 1925, the finance people had restricted the tiny Regular Army to an unviable minimum of arms and equipment, and now, despite the events in Europe, it saw no reason to change. The peacetime army was viewed merely as a force for internal security.

Lt-Gen. M.J. Costello, probably Ireland's most distinguished military leader of the period, who commanded the 1st Thunderbolt Division recollected:

When the war broke out, the main concern was over the ports and the possibility of these being reoccupied by the British. There was also a great deal of anxiety because of Ireland's undertaking to Chamberlain that the ports would be defended and not allowed to fall into any hands hostile to Britain. The strength which Germany or Britain would have to deploy if either invaded went up rapidly from month to month. By 1941, when our forces had grown to 42,000, our response to them would have been formidable ... whereas, in 1939, enemy troops could have landed anywhere in the south and there would have been nothing to stop them. Had they landed in 1941, they would have needed an expeditionary force much larger than Germany used to conquer Norway. After Dunkirk, Gen. Montgomery was ordered to prepare his division to seize Cork Harbour, but he thought the task was unrealistic: he would have needed two divisions but only one could be spared. Of course, if all the British Expeditionary Force had been evacuated from France, it's more than likely Britain would have made an attempt to seize Cork Harbour and Berehaven. For the Germans, the air facilities in the Shannon area would have been more attractive targets than the south coast ports. That is why we established Fort Shannon with guns powerful enough to deal with any naval vessel which might be tempted to come up the estuary.

But was Ireland truly neutral? Its policy was, in fact, very much one-sided and un-neutral. RAF and US aircraft operating in and out of Northern Ireland bases were allowed to fly unhindered in Irish airspace and above territorial waters and navigational markings were placed on the ground especially to assist them. If any crashed or force-landed, surviving crews were given medical care and victims were reverentially treated. The quick and the dead, and the remains of their aircraft, were returned to Northern Ireland, though sometimes the victims were buried locally with full military honours in accordance with the wishes of their next-of-kin. For diplomatic reasons some Allied survivors were subject to periods of liberal internment before being repatriated. The same treatment was given to Luftwaffe survivors but they were kept in internment until the end of the war. Army Intelligence co-operated closely with its British counterpart and the army chiefs had many mutual exchanges with the Allied forces in

A Short Singapore flying-boat of the Royal Air Force moored alongside the Haulbowline Naval Base in Cork Harbour. A trio of these flying-boats visited the harbour in July 1930. Though Britain had certain aviation rights granted in 1922 by the Anglo-Irish Treaty, it never showed any interest in taking these up until the Second World War when this Treaty had been rescinded. The three aircraft provided joyrides for members of the RN guardship and some of the gunners from the forts.

Northern Ireland. Everything was done except a declaration of war on the Axis powers. Behind the bluster of their political masters the top Allied commanders considered that Ireland was more valuable to their cause by virtue of its benevolent neutrality than as a combatant.

Nevertheless, neutral Ireland was very much in the front line. Thousands of men volunteered for the British forces and gave outstanding service, as is recorded in the Royal British Legion's tally of decorations – thousands more were employed in war work in Britain, including the construction of aerodromes. Paradoxically, most of the military volunteers and war-workers fully supported neutrality as it ensured the safety of their loved ones at home. Ireland continued its 'non-combatant' support of the Allied cause to the end; in this she was more honest than other neutral countries which jumped on the victor's bandwagon only when the outcome was assured.

Chapter 19

'Stand to' in the forts

Life for the Irish gunners, being in the midst of their own people, was very different from their predecessors. One of the men who took part in the takeover in the summer of 1938 recollects:

On the day following the hand-over we were given over in four sections to the British sergeant instructors who took us on a tour of Fort Carlisle which had a quite complicated layout. Of course the instructors knew the place intimately and the surrounding area too. They took us from the fort across pasture lands to White Bay which had a lovely sandy beach for swimming and sunbathing. At the end of that day we were given a week's rest on light duties, before full-scale training began. Looking back on those days it is strange to remember that although some of us were almost 19 years of age, not one of us took a drink, we were all teetotallers. But by the time we were 20 we had started taking a modest drop that being all we could afford. All the while that the British NCOs were instructing us, their officers were briefing ours until after about two months we were able to fire the guns by night and by day using dummy rounds.

Two Irish gunners relax with a Guinness
in the company of their mascot in 1939.

Training took up a few hours each day and the rest of our time we were
engaged on various fatigue jobs. I was lucky enough, together with four
of my pals, to be allotted permanent store jobs which kept us off fatigues.
My job entailed checking instruments: the range-finder and position-finder
in their separate locations. I also looked after the huge magazine where I
had to check the temperatures outside and inside and then open or close
ventilators to equalise the readings. Constant high temperature harms
ammunition which had to be shielded from the sun, and given a free circu-
lation of air through it. Moisture too was harmful as it could cause metal
parts of the ammo to rust, and dampen such things as detonators.

An old school pal of mine and many of my other comrades, were notable
sportsmen both in Gaelic football and hurling, and they played for their
various counties, often in opposing teams. We were all delighted when we
found out that a civil engineer from the Board of Works (now the Office

of Public Works) had been a member of Tom Barry's famous West Cork flying column which had played such a prominent part in the War of Independence just 17 years previously. He regaled us with tales of those stirring times. He departed temporarily on the outbreak of war but came back to us in the rank of commandant.

Things changed with the outbreak of the Second World War or 'The Emergency' as it was known, and life became more hectic. When gunners were on duty they slept by the guns instead of in their billets, and during the frequent invasion scares they 'stood to'. By 1942 the army stood at a total of 46,000 all ranks. In that year the two 6-inch guns on Spike Island, together with the battery observation post and the directing station were relocated to give maximum coverage over the harbour. This work was done by two field engineering companies and the subsequent tests of all installations showed everything much improved. Some of the engineers remained to complete a new electric light emplacement and its engine room. The coastal defence engineers came over from Fort Camden and installed new searchlights and switch gear. By June 1943 Spike at last had proper anti-aircraft defences when 40mm and 3.7-inch guns, both mobile types, arrived.

The expanded army had enough coal in stock to carry it through 1941, but then the troops had to turn to the bog for further fuel supplies. Luckily there were plenty of usable bogs which became well known to virtually every soldier, officers included. Every unit was involved, with the adverse effect that training in the summer months could often be interrupted. However, the manual work in the open toughened up the already fit troops. New roads had to be built and bad bogs drained. In the words of an observer, 'I can see those army lads now, in their brown fatigue uniforms, marching along with sleans over their shoulders or pushing wheelbarrows, and singing away.'

Even the coastal gunners on rocky Bere Island had to come ashore

Cavalry troopers and gunners use a gun barrel as a convenient seat in the sun.

to dig their quota. A soldier/sleansman tells the tale:

> Thirty of us arrived at the bog and we saved 300 tons of the stuff, but at
> what a cost. We arrived in a thunderstorm which levelled all our bell tents,
> leaving us wet, cold, and very despondent. But the next day rose up hot and
> sunny and we dried ourselves as best we could because, 'the turf must be
> saved at all costs'. We moved into cattle sheds at a nearby farm where condi-
> tions were primitive – but the turf was finally dry and was taken by lorry
> to the jetty for a barge to bring it out to our island. While waiting for the
> barge, the huge clamp of turf caught fire and very soon was reduced to ashes,
> or had fallen into the sea! From then on we bought turf from Cork County
> Council, thanks be to God, and timber from the Dunboyne Estate.

Meanwhile, up in Donegal, there were some gunners who thought that
a posting to the forts on Lough Swilly was akin to banishment to Siberia,
but mostly the garrisons were happy to be stationed there. One of the

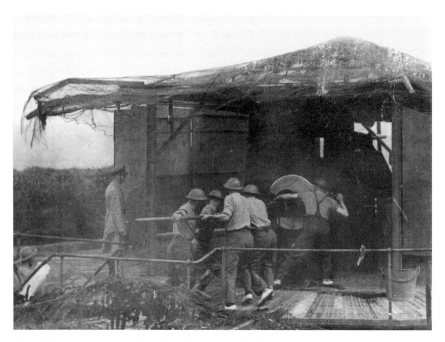

One of the 9.2-inch guns at Fort Templebreedy 'on load' …

… and firing during a practice shoot.

latter was a Wexford man who enjoyed his five years there. Fifty years later he described Dunree as one of the best outposts of the Irish Army:

It was the job of us men from the Corps of Engineers to maintain the water and electricity supply at the forts and to operate the two Crossley engines which supplied power to the searchlights. Payday was Wednesday and in the evening many of us headed off for Buncrana, a holiday resort where two of the favourite local pubs were, The Excelsior and The Dunree Bar.

The town had a band called 'The Rhythm Boys' and they played at St Mary's hall before it was turned into a cinema where we saw many a fine film. The band moved to a new dance hall which was built about 1943. When we felt a bit hungry we could visit Cavanagh's which served up good wholesome meals for a reasonable charge. There was also the Trocadero, if we wanted a cup of tea and a light snack. We could visit Derry City in Northern Ireland on the little narrow gauge railway running from Buncrana, even though the train times did not fit in too well with our time off, we made quite a few trips to that city. Other diversions were the parish hall at Desergetney and McRory's pub close by, both very popular with the lads. One night at the latter, which had extended its hours into the early morning led to me and three comrades being confined to barracks for three days. We made up a story that we happened on a wedding party until the Commandant, half grinning and half scowling, called me a liar and added, 'Whatever they do in the Diocese of Ferns during Lent, we don't have weddings in these parts.'

Another Emergency volunteer had mixed views on being posted to Donegal:

I managed to get myself sent to Dunree out on the Inishowen Peninsula where the garrison was the nearest thing to the Foreign Legion. Our 6-inch guns, built into a kind of Maginot Line emplacement on the hill, looked magnificent. Their shells were lifted out of the magazines with chains and pulleys, and their sinister-looking bagged charges (I always had a fear of explosions) all contrasted with the huge Wagnerian landscape of beautiful Lough Swilly. My duties, after first parade every morning, was to climb the hill and check the Depression Range Finder to know the plus-or-minus rise or fall of the tide which was essential for good gunnery. I became very fond of this beautiful little instrument which, each morning, would tell me that the tide was maybe up 4 feet or down 6 feet. This information was crucial because a target would be up or down those important few feet, indeed on the Irish tides they could be up or down 12 feet. Once, I unscrewed the lenses and breathed on them, polished them thoroughly, and put the whole thing back together again. Next day, however, the instrument revealed that the tide was down by 35 feet. 'Be the holy, there's a fuckin' hole in Lough Swilly', exclaimed our Battery Sergeant. The instrument had to be sent off for checking by the Ordnance Corps. While it was away, a signal announced my promotion to Corporal and I was off to fresh fields before I could be charged with damaging a valuable instrument.

Cork Harbour, 1942. A 'flag-wagger' of the Signal Corps uses a pair of flags to communicate with adjacent forts.

As part of a trickle of supplies from Britain, a pair of 60-pounder guns were accepted by Ireland with the intention of using them for coast defence. However, they were not employed for this purpose and were handed over to an artillery detachment of the Local Defence Force, as seen here. Eventually these unwieldy weapons became static exhibits outside an artillery barracks.

A young officer stationed in Fort Lenan had heard about the fall of Singapore to the Japanese in 1942. He reckoned that had the huge 16-inch coastal defence guns there had the facility of swivelling inwards this might have helped to prevent the disaster when that fortress fell. Prompted by this thought, and ignoring the manuals, he tried to find out how far one of the two 9.2-inch guns could be swung inland. He succeeded in breaking a hydraulic pipe which required a replacement from England. This spare part cost him a month's pay, but by the time it had arrived a skilful 'tiffy' (artificer) had already repaired the damaged item and the unneeded spare was put into store. Years later, when the officer, now a colonel and Director of Artillery was retiring, he was presented with the spare part beautifully mounted on a mahogany base. In the interim, he had learnt to always follow the manual.

Frequent forced landings and crashes by warplanes involved the Lough Swilly garrisons mainly because they were stationed close to the RAF bases in Northern Ireland. The Irish Government had allowed Allied aircraft to use what became known as the 'Donegal corridor' to get into and out of their bases more easily. In all there were forty incidents in Co. Donegal's rugged terrain and its seaboard. In one single week there was a total of seven downed aircraft. The gunners in Dunree and Lenan were involved in twenty of these crashes. A typical accident occurred in April 1941 when a Wellington aircraft on U-boat patrol crashed into the Urris Mountains close to Fort Dunree. On impact, its depth charges exploded, killing all the crew. The 17th Infantry Battalion which guarded the hinterland of the forts had a less tragic experience among the many its men attended. A fighter pilot baled out over Lough Swilly and landed in the water. Getting rid of his parachute he swam to a rock close by and, exhausted, spent the night there. At first light he struck out for the shore and knocked on the door of a cottage, where he was welcomed and given dry clothes, food and drink, and a bed for the night. Next morning, a section from the 17th arrived to take him into custody but the lady of the house told the soldiers tersely, 'Ye cannot take the young man until he has finished his breakfast' – so they had to wait!

Chapter 20

Operating the guns

The most common weapon in the Irish forts was the 6-inch Mk VII land service gun. To operate this weapon there was a crew of two NCOs and seven gunners: most of the team trained solely on actual weapons, except for the four-man loading team. This was because if a shell was loaded into an actual gun it could not be unloaded, it had to be fired. So a dummy loader was used; this was a real breech mounted on a wooden frame and so designed that it retained a dummy shell which had not been properly loaded; it was called a 'ram round' and could be easily retrieved.

In action with a real gun, a crew would act on the orders of the chief NCO who was known as No. 1. Each member of his team were designated by numbers so that his orders could be short and sharp. On the loading team, No.4 was responsible for firing the gun electrically and afterwards he would sponge out the breech to clear it of any burning embers lest a new charge prematurely explode and kill all the gun crew. He was quite a busy number. To load a 6-inch gun required seven separate and swift actions; to achieve this in the shortest possible time called for hours of practice both on the actual gun and on the dummy-loader.

British gunners practice with a dummy loader.

Fire control was at the heart of coast artillery, it made the difference between a devastating hit and just a loud bang. This technique evolved over the years and as advances in both naval design and artillery gathered pace, the coastal gunner had to cope with new problems. He had to engage warships travelling at speed and far out at sea and the old rule-of-thumb methods of laying a gun were useless. In the 1870s a gunner officer came up with solutions in the form of two clever instruments: these were the Depression Range Finder (DRF) and the Position Finder (PF). The DRF, with its telescope laid on the bow of a target, continuously recorded the range as the vessel sped through the water. The PF recorded both range and the bearing of a target far out at sea against which the counter-bombardment 9.2-inch gun would be employed. The vital data received in the observation post would be

Irish gunners load a real 6-inch gun as distinct from a dummy loader.

transmitted directly to the guns where it would be shown on easy-to-read dials for instant action.

The DRF had to be adjusted for changes in the rise or fall of tides and also for atmospheric conditions. These instruments represented a huge advance in fire control when they were introduced in the late nineteenth and the early twentieth century. The DRF worked well up to moderate ranges, but when the longer-range 9.2-inch weapons were engaged in hitting targets miles away, they depended solely on the Position Finder.

The battery commander was responsible for the tactical handling of his guns and for bringing them into action in the shortest possible time. In an observation post, referred to as the 'OP' located some distance from the actual guns, he was assisted by a team of five who operated the fire control instruments. The DRF was located at a known height above the water level. This clever instrument could calculate the

Protected in his concrete command post, a battery commander is taking bearings.

distance to the target by measuring the small angle between itself and the ship. This required careful adjustment for the state of the tides and atmospheric refraction.

There was also long-term data to consider. The rifling in the barrel of a gun would gradually wear out with continuous firing and the weapon's accuracy would suffer. Any changes were recorded carefully and kept in each gun's individual log. This would show the corrections needed by the changing state of the barrel and its knock-on effect on such parameters as temperature, atmospheric pressure and wind, as well as the different types of shells in use. Major calibration tests were always welcomed by the gunners because it gave them an opportunity to fire at least ten full-charge rounds; a rare treat, as ammunition was expensive and sometimes scarce. As the Second World War progressed, early computers appeared and, together with radar, made fire control even more accurate, but these advances were

Beneath the platform of a 9.2-inch gun, a team is laying the weapon on dials, while following instructions from a remote Command Post.

not available in the Irish forts.

The most dedicated field-gunner will acknowledge that the major advances in the art of fire control for every branch of artillery were brought on by developments in coastal gunnery.

Chapter 21

Practice makes perfect

The Latin admonition *si vis pacem, pare bellum* translates as 'If you wish for peace, prepare for war'. Practice at gun-drill was continuous, initially in 1938 under the tutelage of the British instructors with whom a great rapprochement and understanding was developed. These instructors followed the Army way of giving orders in Gaelic – with a strong English accent. Eventually this training would culminate in live firing at targets out at sea. The supplies of ammunition handed over were sparse: there were only 170 rounds for each of the 9.2-inch guns and 275 rounds for each 6-inch gun, with the result that practices with 'full charge' rounds had to be restricted (this means using the maximum amount of propellant). Eventually full charge ammunition was used, first by the guns at Fort Dunree for a night-time shoot. For all annual practices in the North, the target launch *General McHardy* had to be brought around the coast from Berehaven.

North or south, live firing followed the same pattern. About nine miles out a launch, making about 9 knots, would tow target floats strung out on a thousand yards of cable. The length of the floats would be marked out to represent different targets, a battleship, a cruiser, or a destroyer. On the order 'wind in' a winch on the launch would start pulling in the target. The speed of the winch, added to the launch's speed, would cause the targets to travel rapidly, making a dramatic bow wave and a flurry of spray. Now the guns would open up. Any shell which landed within the marked out limits was considered to be a hit on the superstructure or below the vessel's waterline. On board the towing launch an officer operated an instrument known as 'the rake' and readings from this instrument would confirm if a hit had been scored. In time, the gunners became so expert that they could cut the towing cable; this would result in voluble exasperation on the launch because its crew had to rescue the drifting targets, a task which could last till after dark.

In the national press, notices would warn people in the locality of forts to leave their windows open during practices to avoid breakages from blast. A night-time 'shoot' was particularly spectacular for onlookers and thousands would turn out to watch. The whole scene was illuminated by powerful searchlights and any hit by the guns would result in theatrical applause from the audience. The guns on Fort Carlisle were used by the garrisons from all the Cork area forts and it could be said that the sea area here represented a level playing field. In the competition for the Dunboyne Trophy the general standard of a fort, together with the points its gunners scored at the shoots, would result in the award of the trophy – there was strenuous competition to win it.

A retired lieutenant-colonel describes a night shoot when he was a second lieutenant:

> I, being of lowly rank, was sent out to check training in the coast artillery, and the chore could be very pleasant. Seated in the rear of the launch, I manipulated the rake from which I would call out the hits and misses. In 1944 we were detailed to put on a liaison show for General Cunningham, who had just come back from North Africa and was now the British GOC in Northern Ireland – this was to demonstrate how proficient we were in

coast gunnery. This shoot was on Lough Swilly but though we had a very good target-towing ship, as we were coming up from Cork its engine gave trouble off Mayo. But the show had to go on and we impressed a little boat, I will never forget her, called the *Eileen*. A seaman called McGuinness was in charge. So, as darkness fell on Lough Swilly, we cinched up the target but there was only enough cable to pay out for 300 yards, normally the targets were towed about 800 yards behind. A signaller was stationed aft with me to radio my data back to the guns but the Lough was very rough and he got seasick all over my uniform and, whether this affected his signalling or not, the first round took away the rigging of *Eileen*. No doubt the General was impressed. Eventually the target was blown away and we went to retrieve its remains, with me at the controls and McGuinness guiding me. When we reached the shore, this ancient mariner complimented me, a mere landlubber.

Charlie McGuinness deserves a mention. He was born in Derry in 1893 and at the age of fifteen ran away to sea: he sailed around the Horn in a four-masted ship and then served in the Royal Navy before briefly enlisting with the Germans in their African colonies. In Ireland, he played an active part in the War of Independence, including gun-running. Charlie was one of the group in Admiral Byrd's US expedition to Antarctica in 1928 and later published his account of this and his other adventures. Byrd described him as, 'An Irish adventurer of the type that is fast disappearing.'

In 1940, despite being contemptuous of normal discipline and behaviour, Charlie was accepted into the infant Marine Service. When the Taoiseach was inspecting its base at Haulbowline, he was working on a vessel clad in his own version of a naval uniform. Glancing up, he saw Dev and roared out, 'Ah! How are you Eamonn? Haven't seen you in a long time.' De Valera smiled and enquired, 'How are you Charlie?' This great character did not survive for long in the Marine Service: he was arrested and charged with un-neutral conduct involving his

The hazards of being aboard the target-towing launch, graphically illustrated by an unknown artist!

attempts to contact Germany with a radio transmitter. On release from internment after the war, Charlie was in charge of a vessel chartered for a film company. It sank in a violent storm and five members of the crew were lost, including Charlie whose body was never found.

During one night-time shoot on Lough Swilly, a young Donegal midshipman serving on a British battleship observed the pyrotechnics which briefly puzzled him. In later years he remembered:

I have a vivid recollection of that occasion. One night early in August 1943 we were escorting a large troop convoy from Greenock to Casablanca. Whilst on watch, on the first day out from the Clyde, I was on the bridge around midnight when we saw a lot of gun flashes to the south, perhaps 30 miles away, in the direction of Fanad Head. At first it looked as if shipping was under attack. However, almost immediately a signalman came onto the bridge with a wireless report to the effect that the gunfire was from coastal artillery of the Irish Defence Forces and, coming as it was from a neutral country, was to be disregarded. Luckily there were no stray shells!

Chapter 22

Mines and MTBs

Shortly after the Second World War broke out the guardian guns of Cork Harbour were given considerable backup with surface and submarine measures. Just inside the mouth of the harbour and between its two outer forts, a minefield had been sown by the newly organised Marine Service.

Further in, this Service operated a flotilla of six fast motor torpedo boats based at Haulbowline. Block ships were put in position which, when sunk, would further inhibit seaborne invaders.

The Marine Service had a mine-layer which, though not suitable for planting contact mines which Britain was willing to supply, could handle electrically-controlled types. These were tall steel cylinders, filled with explosive, much of which had been salvaged from floating contact mines which frequently broke loose from their moorings and became a hazard when stranded on the shores. The British navy had planted over 6,000 of these off the south-east coast, and the Germans had placed more from U-boats and aircraft. The controlled mines were fabricated at Thompson's Metal Works in Kilkenny and the Great Southern Railways works at Inchicore. Cork Harbour was sown with

A trio of MTBs exercising off Bere Island in 1943.

these mines planted in a stretch of water called Turbot Bank. These were planted 120ft apart at varying depths. On the Carlisle bank a sighting point was established abreast of the minefield where lookouts could alert a control point in the shadow of that fort to approaching dangers. Mines were also laid in the approaches to Waterford harbour and alongside the deep water quay at Cobh.

The motor torpedo boats' (MTBs) role was to dash out to attack belligerent vessels in hit-and-run sorties. Each had four powerful main engines delivering a speed of 40 knots. Despite their limited sea-going capability, these craft went everywhere: destroying floating mines, saving lives, and patrolling the Shannon estuary and its transatlantic flying-boat base at Foynes. But their prime duty was to be on station if Cork Harbour was threatened.

The coastal guns had a subsidiary but very important function, that of supporting a port examination system operated by the Marine Service: independent 12-pounder guns were also installed to provide

Members of 'The 12-Pounder Battery' exercising on this type of gun, located at Sandycove. Independent from coast defence batteries, this unit was established in June 1941 to provide backup for the Marine Service's examination vessels. Manpower only was used to train this light quick-firing weapon.

this clout at Dublin Bay, Waterford and elsewhere. Every vessel about to enter harbour had to be checked for contraband. They would be signalled to stop at designated points and if this was ignored a vessel would be warned by a particularly loud and smoky blank round. If this display did not halt the oncoming ship, the proverbial 'shot across the bows' was delivered as a final warning that the *coup-de-grace* would follow. At night three red lights was the stop signal and if a ship still came on, a Morse lamp would flash 'Oscar Lima', meaning, 'heave to, or I will open fire'. When the vessel complied it would then be directed to an examination area illuminated by searchlights and covered by the guns.

When a vessel hove to in the examination area, a Marine Service launch would be sent out with a boarding party – sometimes there could be a humorous side to this operation. Chief Petty Officer, the Honourable Patrick Campbell, despite his stutter, was given command of the tug *Noray* in Dublin Bay. Crewed by six men who worked in eight-hour watches, each watch was rationed to a small quantity of tea. Tea was like gold dust in wartime Ireland. Thus, when a boarding party was setting out, Campbell would detail one member to go straight to the galley and negotiate with the cook. Once, a gigantic liner provided the prospect of a real killing in tea supplies, but when the boarding party returned Campbell remembered, 'I noticed one lad's jersey bulging with what I took to be an unusually large haul of tea, but it was four bottles of liqueur and, judging by his bemused appearance, he had about the same amount inside him!'

The 'flagship' of the infant Marine Service was a venerable vessel built in Dublin in 1908, as a fisheries protection craft named *Helga*. In the Great War the Royal Navy took her over as an armed yacht and used its gun to shell the General Post Office during the Easter Rising. Afterwards, she sank a German U-boat before returning to her fishery duties. Following the Treaty, and still bearing a white star on the funnel to mark her naval victory, she was renamed *Muirchu* meaning 'Hound of the Sea'. When she entered naval service once again her small gun was replaced by a 12-pounder from one of the forts. On one occasion she could well have been a victim of that very fort when a battery on Bere Island, failing to recognise the vessel, signalled, 'Stop, or I will open fire'. There were a few tense moments but no gunfire. One of the MTBs had a more dramatic escape on its delivery voyage from the UK. Though flying a huge Irish tricolour she was bombed by a pair of German aircraft and suffered a couple of near misses. She returned to the UK to have this damage repaired and then set out again. However, nearing the Irish coast, one of the forts at Cork Harbour didn't correctly identify her and fired, but spotted the mistake before further damage could be done. With friends like those, who needed enemies!

The ports could have been further protected by an offer to the Marine Service of four destroyers: because of strict wartime censorship this story never got out. The Royal Swedish Navy needed reinforcement to properly protect its country's neutrality. Italy, also neutral in the early days of

Mine shells at Thompson's metalworking factory in Kilkenny. These steel casings were fabricated for electrically-operated mines which were sown in Cork Harbour and Waterford. The casings were filled with high explosive, much of it salvaged from the large number of floating mines which were stranded on the Irish coasts.

1940, had four destroyers for sale which the Swedes purchased but their long voyage home was not without incident. With their mother ship *Patricia*, the destroyers arrived at Naples for minor repairs and thereafter they were dogged by a series of problems, including a collision.

Six weeks elapsed before the flotilla arrived under the guns of Cork Harbour, looking for fuel supplies which, due to wartime conditions, were unavailable. Despite this, the flotilla then travelled up north to the Faroe Islands which Britain had taken over to forestall the Germans who had invaded Denmark. Then, in an act of unbelievable piracy, the British Navy took over the neutral ships and with prize crews on board, sailed them to its naval base at Scapa Flow in the Orkneys. Anchored here, the Swedish crews and their ships were subjected to scandalous behaviour by the British sailors, there was widespread vandalism and theft. Intense diplomatic activity ensued.

In the midst of this brouhaha a retired British rear-admiral of Irish extraction appeared in Dublin. Though apparently acting in a private capacity he claimed that he could arrange for the sale by Britain of the Swedish ships at a purely nominal price. He could also arrange for the transfer of trained Irish-born naval personnel to man them. Obviously, the British were offering Ireland a virtual gift of the interned Swedish ships which they, the British, now wanted to purchase from the real owners, for less than half the amount already paid to the Italians. The Irish Government pointed out that it could neither man, operate nor maintain such vessels, even if Britain could provide a legitimate bill-of-sale. This whole bizarre episode underlined Britain's determination following the collapse of France, to prevent these warships falling into German hands, though Sweden had given assurances that this would never happen. Throughout the whole episode Britain's behaviour was in direct contravention of international law but this may have been motivated by the pious hope that the hijacked vessels could be used to defend the Irish coast as there was now an imminent threat of a German invasion of both countries.

An interesting footnote to the above; the naval captain John Fitzgerald, who attempted to sell the ships had been, at the beginning of the war, an advisor to the Irish Government on its infant Coast Watching Service. At that time he had advised against the purchase of motor torpedo boats, stressing that this type of craft would be unsuitable in the sea conditions prevailing around Ireland. Subsequently, as the Marine Service discovered in heavy weather, he had been absolutely right.

Winston Churchill had no qualms about offending Sweden. In fact, he had planned to breach its neutrality with an invasion designed to capture the country's unique capability of producing ball-bearings. Though little known, this 'adventure' is well documented.

Chapter 23

Churchill and the Treaty Ports

It is often said that the first casualty in war is the truth. During the Second World War, nowhere was this more evident than in the anti-Irish propaganda spread by Britain regarding the Irish Treaty ports and forts. It was led by the Prime Minister Winston Churchill, who was described as, 'a rumbling volcano, always liable to erupt over the loss of the ports'. He maintained that the 'so-called neutrality of the so-called Éire' could possibly help Germany by refuelling its U-boats which, after two weeks of the war, had sunk twenty-eight British ships. The more the war at sea went against the British, the angrier Churchill became. He now asked if Éire could be legally regarded as a neutral state and queried if Irish neutrality could be regarded as the neutrality of say Holland or Switzerland? He asked further, what was the international judicial status of Éire? Was it not a dominion? It is certainly under the British Crown. He had conveniently forgotten the agreement of 1938.

Churchill believed Éire was 'at war but skulking'. In fact, legally, whether Éire was a dominion or not, was of no importance: other actual dominions were under no legal obligation to go to war on the side of the mother country. The Dominion of Newfoundland, which had suffered appalling casualties for a small nation in the Great War, had grave reservations about joining in.

Sir John Maffey, the British representative in Ireland, pointed out to Churchill that the policy of neutrality commanded widespread approval among all classes and interests. He said, 'It is remarkable even that the pro-British group, men who had fought for the Crown and are anxious to be called up again, men whose sons are at the front today, Loyalists in the old sense of the word, agreed generally in supporting the policy of neutrality in Eire.'

As the U-boats were increasingly successful, the British public was alarmed and when Churchill needed a whipping boy on whom to lay the blame, he picked on Ireland. Actually the blame lay with the government's pre-war neglect and Churchill's own strategic errors after he became Prime Minister. Churchill was on his feet in the House of Commons, maintaining 'the fact that we cannot use the south and west coasts of Ireland to refuel our flotillas and aircraft, and thus protect the trade by which Ireland as well as Britain lives, is a most heavy and grievous burden, and one which should never have been placed on our shoulders, broad though they be'. But where were these phantom flotillas? They just didn't exist.

Churchill's posturing generated further anti-Irish sentiment which was echoed in the press with cartoons and editorials. Even a rational journal, *The Economist* stated:

> If the ports have become a matter of life and death, for Ireland as well as England, there can be only one way out - we must take them. That would of course revive all the old bitterness. But if bitterness there must be, let us have bitterness and the bases, not the bitterness alone, which is all mere 'retaliation' would provoke.

The war of words continued: even Irishman George Bernard Shaw gently saying that perhaps Ireland should 'loan' the ports and then gently protest when England took them over. Everybody got in on the act, politicians, diplomats, poets and historians. The foreign secretary, Anthony Eden, had this to say in his memoirs, 'No minor contrivance could compensate for the loss of the Irish ports and of Berehaven in particular. The Agreement of 25 April 1938 had surrendered their use, and the resultant toll in ships and lives was to be cruel and hard to bear.' This was wrong, especially coming from a man who a few years after the war had connived with France and Israel to invade Egypt, a neutral country – with disastrous results which ended his political career.

Lord Ismay, the senior British military adviser to the War Cabinet, made the astounding claim that the ports had been denied, '… despite promises which the Irish Government made when we handed them over in April 1938'. No such promises were ever made and do not appear anywhere in the Agreement. In his diary Sir Wilfred Spender recorded, 'the lack of the ports had led to the loss, so I am told, of hundreds of ships and some thousands of lives'. One wonders who told him that? Nicholas Monserrat, in his best-selling book, *The Cruel Sea*, wrote:

> To compute how many men and how many ships this denial was costing, month after month, was hardly possible, but the total was substantial and tragic. From these bases, the Battle of the Atlantic might have been fought on something like equal terms. As it was, the bases were denied; escorts had to go the long way round to get to the battlefield and return to the harbour at least two days earlier than would have been necessary; the cost, in men and ships, added months to the struggle and ran up a score which Irish eyes a-smiling on the day of Allied victory were not going to cancel.

This was a calumny totally at odds with reality. Louis MacNiece, a Belfast poet (the centenary of whose birth was marked nationally in 2007), was equally damning in his poem 'Neutrality' with the lines, 'While to the west off your own shores the mackerel are fat – on the flesh of your kin'. Yet another author (Roskill), writing on the Atlantic

War, maintained that Britain had to give up the use of the south-western Atlantic approaches because of Ireland's intransigence.

Palpable rubbish, as any British naval strategist can confirm.

This virulent propaganda, totally at odds with the facts, continued to damage Ireland for many years after the war and persists to the present. In 1970 the British historian Max Beloff wrote, 'It is quite clear that the Irish deliberately led the British and other Commonwealth people to believe that they would be with them if war came against Nazi Germany, and that therefore the ports could be safely surrendered to their keeping.' One can only ask, when? Beloff added, 'Having got the ports they [the Irish] proceeded on the road towards a neutrality, tragic not only for Britain but also for all the nations of the anti-Hitler coalition.' Did Beloff ever read the 1938 Agreement or think of modifying his remarks by listing Ireland's heavy pro-Allied neutrality? Also he forgot to mention that initially there was no anti-Hitler coalition, and that America, Russia, and a whole scad of European nations were solidly neutral until they were invaded.

Occasionally, Irish academics propose a case for their country joining the Allies. What these latter-day pundits fail to understand is that the Irish people, having achieved a measure of freedom, had subsumed their neutrality into long-awaited sovereignty. Many armchair experts have continually failed to understand 'the times that were in it'. This strong and overwhelming feeling is crucial in understanding the situation in 1939. It should also be remembered that throughout the war, in Great Britain as well as Ireland, the general public was almost completely unaware of Nazi atrocities. At the end, when details of the Holocaust emerged, both nations were shocked to the core.

Wartime propaganda continued to denigrate Ireland's neutral stance, even though the conflict had ended. But now, with the availability of many restricted documents, the realities could be calmly analysed. One such was a letter written in July 1940 by Admiral Max Horton who asked:

> Do the people realise that with the enemy air force based along the French coast, no Channel routes can be used, and that the whole of the southern approaches between Land's End and Ireland will shortly be controlled by enemy aircraft? That route, up to now our principal route for supplies, will probably have to be abandoned …

So much for the strategic value of Cork Harbour and Berehaven.

One British naval historian highlighted the problems created by muddled thinking and neglect between the wars:

> The indecisive Battle of Jutland in 1916 befogged the Royal Navy's thinking over the entire horizon of maritime warfare in the years before the Second World War, and not just with regard to the design of destroyers or the relative importance of battleships or aircraft carriers. The role of the British submarine service, for its part, was seen merely as ancillary to the operations of the battlefield … but far more dangerous was the Admiralty's parallel neglect of the potential threat to Britain's survival posed by enemy submarines. The neglect, or rather, minimising it, was truly remarkable … The navy in the 'twenties and 'thirties chose to believe that technical progress in the performance of Sonar [the system whereby enemy submarines could be audibly located] would greatly lessen the effectiveness of the submarine as a weapon against shipping.

This was a forlorn hope.

Post-war, the Naval Staff History of Trade Defence observed:

> The fact remains that in the inter-war period the Royal Navy never undertook any systematic examination and analysis of the course of the war waged against Allied shipping in the course of the First World War. At no time was there any study that related the number of operational U-boats to

the number of merchantmen which they sank, and there was no analysis of the role of anti-submarine units at the time when they made kills. There was no attempt to examine the loss of time and tonnage imposed by independent routing of merchantmen, nor was there any attempt to examine the implications of the fact that in the First World War the number of ships sailing in convoy and the number of U-boats sunk, both increased at much the same rate.

A critical ratio in any new war.

In peacetime, career-minded officers could see no clear way to promotion if they specialised in anti-submarine warfare. Indeed, the future of many regular naval officers was blighted by the application of the Geddes Axe in 1926 which made many redundant and left them 'on the beach'. In those years a great reliance had been placed on the convoy system but there were two other glaring deficiencies, that of proper escorts and maritime aircraft. In 1937, when the British re-armament programme rather belatedly got under way, the Admiralty began to build what it hoped would be a new, robust, simple and cheap escort vessel, the Hunt Class destroyer. This hope was not realised because these vessels were over-designed, expensive and not suitable for North Atlantic conditions. A far better escort vessel for Atlantic conditions, the Corvette, was then developed but orders were not placed until just before the outbreak of war for 246 of this sturdy but uncomfortable vessel. Part of this order was completed in 1940 and the balance in 1941. Muddle and delay caused two years to be lost and this left the navy dangerously lacking essential escort vessels during the initial period of the war. These were the phantom flotillas, which Winston Churchill was so keen to base in the Treaty ports.

Of course, the new Atlantic battle would be fought out in mid-ocean and the Irish bases were of no importance compared to Plymouth and Portsmouth. In the Great War the Irish ports had undoubtedly played an important role as bases for large numbers of destroyers and other escorts. But the sea battle of that time had been fought at short range in the south-western approaches, whereas in the Second World War the conflict was fought at long range and naval strategy had changed completely.

In fact, Churchill had become almost paranoid about Ireland to the unease of some of his cabinet colleagues. The War Cabinet was stunned when in September 1943 he announced that he proposed now during the war to solve the Irish problem. His cabinet colleagues reacted with dismay and one of his most loyal supporters, Leo Amry, wrote that Churchill withdrew his proposals:

> … with not too good a grace … I am afraid that unless he draws in his horns … we shall be in for trouble, both in Ireland and internally here in the cabinet … I have always been afraid that at some point Winston might lose his balance and it may be that this is the one.

It seemed as if paranoia had set in. Even after the successful Allied invasion of France, a time when Ireland was of no possible strategic importance, a MI5 officer noted that Churchill seemed to have a continuous bee in his bonnet about Ireland, whose neutrality he, Churchill, regarded as a personal affront.

In summary, it was Britain's own neglect which almost brought that country to the verge of starvation. Possession of the Irish Treaty ports could not have improved Britain's naval strategy in any way. Had the Treaty ports been made available to Britain, the only outcome would have been that not only would they have been attacked by Germany, but the rest of the country would have suffered. Ireland could not have defended herself against a strong air and naval onslaught. This fact was exemplified by Britain's neglect of the defences in its Northern Ireland bailiwick which was clearly demonstrated by the two air raids on Belfast in 1941.

The above is not an apologia for Ireland's neutrality: rather it sets out the realities of 'The Battle of the Atlantic'. Far more crucial than the Irish ports in that campaign was Churchill's neglect when he was First Lord of the Admiralty and his misguided 'adventures' when he became Prime Minister in 1940; all left the Royal Navy without the vessels it needed in the Atlantic.

Chapter 24

The Fort on the Shannon

The story of the Treaty ports and forts represents what Britain continues to regard as 'non-co-operation' or in some ways, treachery by her erstwhile dominion, so perhaps it is legitimate to describe a case where both countries co-operated. The estuary of Ireland's great river, the Shannon, had been fortified during the Napoleonic wars when a number of batteries and guard houses were built on each bank with Co. Clare on the north, and Co. Kerry on the south. Two of these defences had existed on the southern shore close to the town of Tarbert, but the estuary had not been fortified prior to the Great War because it was not considered a sufficiently deep anchorage for the Fleet, despite being navigable for lesser vessels all the way up to Limerick City.

Urged on by Britain, Ireland decided to protect the estuary at a place called Ardmore Point about fifteen miles from the sea because further upstream at Foynes lay the transatlantic terminus of the flying-boat service between its island and the seaport. On the North American side the terminus was at Botwood in Canada and Foynes became a vital strategic link for the Allies. When VIP passengers and war material arrived at Foynes, all were transported to Rineanna, a modern international airport in Clare in clear breach of 'neutrality'. Until the invasion of France in 1944, Foynes and Rineanna jointly represented the only safe staging post for air traffic between the UK and America, the Mediterranean, and the Middle and Far East.

Two coastal guns were required to protect these facilities against an attack by surface raiders or submarines. The Irish Government felt that Berehaven was not an important base and suggested that the two 6-inch guns mounted in Lonehort Battery should be poached and used to equip the new installation, called Fort Shannon. But the Royal Navy, still harbouring the hope that Berehaven might somehow, sometime, be available to it, was reluctant to see these guns moved. Being well aware of the advantages to Britain of both air bases, Churchill, who would only allow the minimum military equipment for Éire, now agreed to provide a pair of 6-inch Mk VII guns on naval mountings. These weapons had been fabricated in 1902/3 but were still considered to be efficient, modern weapons. Though there were wartime shortages in Ireland, the basic material for construction came in abundance from the cement works at Limerick and Dundalk, and from many gravel pits. The army had already used this supply liberally when placing tons of concrete for pillboxes, tank traps, bunkers, field fortifications, underground headquarters and roads.

The site for the new fort was well chosen. Any surface raider moving up the Shannon, without prior intelligence, would have been unaware of the presence of the guns until it was negotiating the navigable channel some miles from the fort. At this point it would have been restricted in its ability to manoeuvre and could only have brought its forward guns to bear in self-defence. The guns and the searchlights in the fort were so positioned to give an element of surprise. By clever use of the terrain, the guns were on rising ground but then the terrain changed to conceal the power houses, cable trunking, and communications links rendering the fort invisible to the intruder.

Construction of the new fort began in August 1942; two gun houses

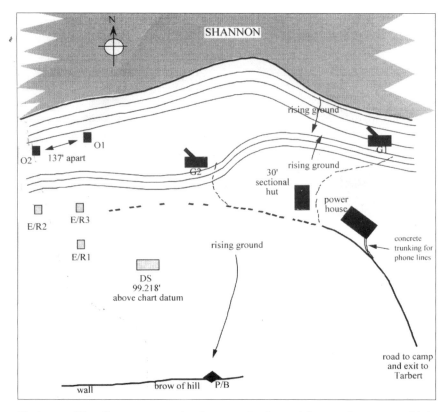

The layout of Fort Shannon as completed in 1942. On the top left, O1 and O2 are searchlight posts for which the three positions marked E/R provided electricity. The position marked D/S is the Director Station and is combined with the Battery Operating Position. The Power House seen on the right provided overhead electrical supply to the camp which lay further over to the right and included accommodation and messing facilities in standard wooden huts. At the bottom of the map, P/B was the site of one of the machine-gun posts which gave and all-round field of fire which, together with five other machine-gun posts, were designed to deter an attack by a landing party or by supporters of 'an illegal organisation'.

were built, one close to the water on the forward slope of a slight hill and a second higher up behind it. Ancillary buildings were put in position: magazines, searchlights, powerhouses, and three small brickwork engine rooms to deliver power to the searchlights. Each gun-house led to a tunnel and underground magazines. These were some distance behind each gun, which meant that shells had to be carried to the 'ready-to-use' lockers

The reinforced concrete emplacement for No.1 gun still stands close to the bank of the River Shannon.

in the gun-houses. The landward side of the new fort was defended by six Vickers machine-guns, housed in pillboxes, while the hinterland was patrolled by 'the Bikes', three cyclist squadrons from the Cavalry Corps.

Four hundred men of the Seventh and Eighth Field Companies of the Corps of Engineers, assisted by a company of lads from the Construction Corps, undertook the work. All progressed speedily, with the exception of one hiccup with the first gun. An engineer officer of the time tells how it occured:

> We were ready to install the guns which came to us in three main pieces – the barrel, the cradle, and the pedestal, with an all up weight of over 16 tons. The pedestal sat on a 6 foot deep reinforced concrete bed to which it was secured by a circle of 22 long anchor bolts. An officer was despatched to a depot in Dublin to check on these which turned out to be 3 feet 10 inches long and they were set precisely in the concrete with their shanks protruding, ready for the guns. By the time these arrived, the concrete had fully set and hardened around the bolts.
>
> Using heavy tackle and muscle power, the pedestal base was lowered onto the bolts followed by the gun cradle and barrel. We then moved in to fit and

tighten large securing nuts onto the protruding shanks but, to our horror, there was insufficient thread on some of the bolts! As we wrestled with this predicament, a bombshell exploded in the form of a signal from headquarters saying that at 0830 hrs the next day the Chief-of-Staff, the Director of Engineering, and other assorted top brass would be paying us a visit.

Something had to be done – and quickly. The gun was inched upwards until it was 2 feet clear, putting chocks in all the while to take the weight off the lifting equipment. Then thirty-two wielders of hammer and chisel set to work in teams of eight: chipping away at the rock-hard concrete to a depth of 1½ inches over all of the 6 foot circle. As dawn broke, blood oozed from many bruised, tired and unbandaged hands. At 4.30 in the morning the base had been chipped away to the required level, and the complete gun was put back in position. Sharp at 0830 hours, two staff cars pulled up at the site and out came the Chief-of-Staff. It was all over in a few minutes: a quick walk around the gun; a sharp laconic comment by the Chief, 'I see nothing wrong with this bloody gun' – and all departed.

But what had gone wrong initially? Well, it happened through the common, natural error of taking things for granted. The officer who had gone to the depot, accurately measured one bolt and naturally assumed that all were the same length – but a half dozen were short. This dilemma was compounded by the necessity to work to precise levels at the gun site. The incident reinforced a lesson: the requirement to check and re-check everything.

Despite the early hiccup the work was completed in four months and handed over to the gunners in November 1942.

In practice shoots over the broad reaches of the Shannon estuary the guns demonstrated that they were a formidable pair, as did the gunners who rescued the crew when a vessel capsized nearby. Few traces remain of Fort Shannon, but after the war its two guns were despatched to Fort Dunree where they now stand guard in front of the museum.

Chapter 25

New Names, Old Problems, Future Hopes

The Treaty forts had borne the names of British VIPs throughout their long history, until 1951. Now they commemorate the leaders of the Young Ireland movement of the nineteenth century. Fort Carlisle became Fort Davis after the poet and nationalist Thomas Davis (1840-1871). Davis had been born in Mallow, Co. Cork, educated at Trinity College, Dublin and called to the bar in 1838. He joined the Repeal Association with Daniel O'Connell on the issue of non-denominational education and then became unofficial leader of the Young Irelanders. Davis was a major literary and political influence on his contemporaries. He wrote many popular ballads, including, 'A Nation Once Again'. He died in Dublin when he was only thirty-one, and his funeral was a major public event.

Fort Camden became Fort Meagher in memory of Thomas Frances Meagher (1823-1867) from Waterford. As a Member of Parliament he delivered an inflammatory speech which gave him the name 'Meagher of the Sword'. He is closely associated with the

Cocooned at Carlisle. A battery of 12-pounders used for saluting visiting vessels. Spike Island can be seen in the background.

green, white. and orange tricolour of the Republic, which was based on that of revolutionary France. For his part in the ill-fated Rising of 1848 he was transported to Van Diemen's Land but he escaped to the United States where he led an Irish brigade for the Union in some of the bloodiest battles of the Civil War. When he was acting Governor of Montana he drowned mysteriously in the Missouri River. The flag of his brigade was returned to Ireland by President Kennedy in 1962.

The fort on Spike Island was initially called Fort Westmoreland but this was changed to honour John Mitchel. He was born in Co. Derry, the son of a Unitarian minister, and educated at Trinity College, Dublin. A solicitor, he wrote many editorials for *The Nation* which became the more radical *United Irishman*. In 1848 he was held on Spike Island where he wrote his famous *Jail Journal*, before being transported for treason-felony to Van Diemen's Land. In 1853 he too escaped to the United States where he supported the Confederacy. He returned to Ireland and was twice elected as a Member of Parliament for Co. Tipperary. The other Treaty forts continue to be known by their geographical locations: Lenan, Dunree, Berehaven, and Templebreedy, this being a corruption of the Gaelic name for St Bridget's church.

After the Second World War when conventional coastal defence from fixed bases became outmoded, the Dept of Defence agreed to hand over Fort Camden to the Cork County Council. At a ceremony in May 1989, the Minister said that the government was delighted that the history of the fort, which seemed to be coming to an end, would now continue to unfold, and would make a major contribution to the development of tourism in the region. The Minister confirmed that 'one of the attractions will be a display of the torpedo system developed in 1852 by the Co. Mayo inventor Louis Brennan'. The County Council confirmed that it would turn the ancient fort into a military museum with an interpretative centre and a restaurant for tourists with beautiful harbour views.

Shortly before this event a party from the International Fortress Study Group visited the fort and its journal reported as follows:

> There is a zig-zag ramp with hauling rings and two very long stepped passageways, all leading to the water-level batteries … a slowly rising passage leads to four armoured 11-inch RML casemates, complete with mantlet bars … in the open there are three pre-Great War 12-pounder positions … through a massive portal, two piers and a quay with a Brennan torpedo position can be seen … using the 18-inch gauge track on the quay, a locomotive would be lifted by crane to the higher level. Care was taken over safety: the quay floor was 'pecked', passage floors were crosshatched, and the stairs were of granite. The most beautiful of these led to the magazines; wedge-shaped and cantilevered out from the walls of the

circular shaft without centre support, they spiralled glistening up from the darkness.

A glowing report and an incidental tribute to the poor convicts who had built the fort?

After the handover ceremony, a development plan for the lower levels of the fort was proposed by the remaining army detachment, the 8th Field Artillery Regiment. This unit was designated as a co-ordinator for all interested parties: Cork County Council, Cork/Kerry Tourism, and Bord Fáilte (the Irish Tourist Board). The plan would run as follows:

> There will be three phases: the first to begin in August 1987 for completion by the end of that year; phase two will begin in January 1988 for completion by November; and the final phase will commence in January 1989 for completion by the end of the year. Each phase will be supported by a detailed work study with itemised costing prepared by qualified personnel. The time span between phases can be telescoped or lengthened as the situation demands. Funding of the project will be the subject of a separate annex.

In February 1987 the officer commanding the co-ordinating unit wrote:

> The upper levels will be used for the foreseeable future as storage for Southern Command and as a training location for the FCA and Sluagh Muiri [army and naval reserves respectively]. The lower levels are of immense historical value and must be preserved. This would be best carried out by appropriate agencies under military direction, making full use of all material within the state.

This development plan made perfect sense, but nothing, absolutely nothing, was implemented. Thus, in 2008, Fort Meagher, the finest example of its type in Europe, continues to deteriorate into a ruin, battered by the elements.

The neglect of this Treaty fort and of its twin, Fort Davis, and other significant military installations throughout the country, contrasts with other European countries which cherish historical military installations such as coastal forts and have transformed many into first-class visitor centres and museums, as has been the case at Fort Dunree in Donegal.

The Fort Dunree Heritage Museum complex, initially opened to the public in 1986, is a shining example of what can be done, in contrast to the neglect of the Cork forts. It has proved a great attraction for tourists of all ages and numbers are increasing from a current base of 10,000 per annum. There is a video film presentation in the theatre and the museum itself displays what is regarded as the finest collection anywhere of coastal defence artefacts and images. The underground bunkers also have a collection which gives meaning and insight into the operation of the fort in its heyday. The museum is unique in that all the guns and equipment on view there represent the greatest collection of coast defence weaponry in the latter part of the nineteenth century, with the exception of the 9.2-inch gun.

The only state-aided military preservation work in Ireland is under the supervision of the National Parks and Monuments Branch of the Office of Public Works. Work is under way at two sites in Kinsale; Charles Fort, the most important artillery fort of the late seventeenth century and the earlier artillery fort, James's Fort, at Castle Park. The future of the Treaty forts, still extant, depends ultimately on public awareness and on the involvement of local and state-aided agencies for their restoration and conservation. They are part of Ireland's history and heritage.

Fort Dunree is set in a spectacular natural area rich in wildlife unique to the area and this is further highlighted in the museum which has a beautiful wildlife exhibition with sea life and bird life displays. Recent developments at Dunree include a network of sign-posted paths with spectacular views which can be explored at leisure. There are detailed information boards, shelters, picnic tables and a new waterfront cafeteria. One asks, 'If it can be done in Donegal, why not in Cork Harbour too?'